T0165939

OTHER BOOKS BY EVA SAULITIS

Prayer in Wind

Leaving Resurrection:
Chronicles of a Whale Scientist

Many Ways to Say It

Into Great Silence:
A Memoir of Discovery and Loss in the
Realm of Vanishing Orcas

Becoming
EARTH

essays

Eva Saulitis

Book design and layout by Selena Trager

Library of Congress Cataloging-in-Publication Data
Names: Saulitis, Eva, 1963–2016
Title: Becoming earth / Eva Saulitis.
Description: First edition. | Pasadena, CA : Boreal Books, 2016.
Identifiers: LCCN 2015048442 | ISBN 9781597099035 (casebound) | ISBN
9781597099110 (paperback : alkaline paper)
Subjects: LCSH: Saulitis, Eva, 1963—Health. | Saulitis, Eva,
1963—Philosophy. | Breast—Cancer—Patients—United States—Biography. |
Metastasis—Patients—United States—Biography. | Women authors,
American—Biography. | Cancer—Psychological aspects. |
Death—Psychological aspects. | Mortality—Psychological aspects. |
Mortality—Philosophy. | Philosophy of nature.
Classification: LCC RC280.B8 S274 2016 | DDC 362.19699/4490092—dc23
LC record available at http://lccn.loc.gov/2015048442

The Los Angeles County Arts Commission, the National Endowment for the
Arts, the Pasadena Arts & Culture Commission and the City of Pasadena
Cultural Affairs Division, the Los Angeles Department of Cultural Affairs,
Dwight Stuart Youth Fund, Sony Pictures Entertainment, and the Ahmanson
Foundation partially support Red Hen Press.

First Edition
Published by Boreal Books
an imprint of Red Hen Press, Pasadena CA
www.borealbooks.org
www.redhen.org

for Craig

Contents

ONE

TWO

All words about death are a lie, since all hopes are a lie. Words are futile hopes.

A clump of earth, a stone, a greedy strip of green: these don't lie.

—Anna Kamienska

ONE

In the Body That Once Was Mine

MY BODY MATURED ON THE floodplain of Lake Erie, weather maker, nearly ten thousand square miles of freshwater surface area upon which winds kick up violent waves. I grew up on its eastern shore, fifty miles south of Buffalo, in the rural village of Silver Creek, surrounded by vineyards and apple orchards, with a population of only twenty-five hundred. Its once-vital Main Street, where my parents could buy our shoes, clothes, fabric, groceries, hardware, jewelry, notions, toys, gifts, and greeting cards, was eroded gradually by the building of malls in the suburbs of Buffalo, then by the demise of the steel industry in nearby Lackawana.

Lake effect, the winter storms off Lake Erie are called. Before it freezes solid in winter, the lake's open water is the mother of epic snows that shut down schools and close Interstate 90 for days. After the blizzard of '77, we returned to high school after a week of snow days to a building entombed, the windows whited out completely by twelve-foot-high drifts. Having now lived half my life on the Gulf of Alaska, it's weird to say, but true: Lake Erie could be untamed, wild, a shape-shifter. Midwinter, it froze into a sastrugi-chiseled white expanse, the shoreline berg-choked. In late fall, gray skies turned the lake leaden. In summer, it could be strangely lit by heat lightning, by thunderheads, by a yellow humid haze. Or it could be baby blue and benign, dull and flat, a smudged smoke-blue suggestion of Canada visible only on clearest days. As a child, it formed my horizon: sometimes violent, often dull, and in its own way, mythic. Playing in overhead waves jostled up by a day breeze, I feared the lamprey eels my brothers claimed could latch onto my legs and bore bloody holes all the way to the bone. On hot summer days, my mother would take us to a beach where we'd get sunburned picking through a wrackline of eelgrass, sticks, and plastic bits, searching for weathered glass, breathing in the ammonia stench of dead carp and small fish called pumpkinseeds, their eyeless, dried-out corpses half-buried in sand. The lake built the bounds I imagined for my childhood desires—water badly used, once declared dead, water resurrected. I hardly envisioned a life for myself out of its gaze until college, when I saw a film about wolves in the far north. A few months before leaving for Alaska, at twenty-one, I walked the winter shore of Erie one last time with a friend, our faces wrapped in wool scarves to protect us from a bitter wind. The whole lake that day was a white plain of snow-covered ice, edged along the beach by a scrim of dirty jumbled berg sculptures as tall as our heads. I saw the lake that day for what it was, at heart, what it had once been—a wild place. Its name originates from the Iroquois word for "long tail" (mountain lion)—those cats having once inhabited the region—to reflect its unpredictable nature. Before, I'd imagined ice like that only in my Alaskan dream.

Growing up, to me the lake, despite its storms, was the opposite of wilderness, tainted by its association with industry, death, and degradation. Even now, for anyone older than fifty, its name is synonymous with pollution and shipwreck. For others, it's associated with recreation—with summer cottage life in places like Sunset and Hanover and Hanford Bay, with the beach bar scene where my friends and I got drunk after we turned eighteen, with snow cone stands, with speedboats pulling water skiers or carrying partiers dressed as pirates from bar to bar, with pike and steelhead fishing (though we ate only a limited number of those fish, due to toxic contamination).

Lake Erie is the shallowest of the Great Lakes, its mean depth only sixty-two feet, yet it's the thirteenth largest lake in the world in terms of surface area. In places I could wade out a quarter mile and not get my chest wet. After sewage dumping and farm runoff and steel plant effluent were controlled, the lake cleaned up dramatically during my childhood due to that shallowness, the winds turning the water from top to bottom, over and over. Yet as we now know, some pollution persists long after it is banned from use. DDT, illegal since 1972, sometimes wells up from the lake's basin, where it's held in sediments. It can still be found in the flesh of predator fish, along with PCBs. Even now, a dead, oxygenless zone forms every summer somewhere in the lake, like an embodied memory of abuse, like silence.

I witnessed sources of that abuse during childhood on drives to Buffalo to visit my parents' immigrant Latvian friends, the thruway taking us through the steel mill town of Lackawanna, with its spewing stacks and grimed-up row houses. *Lackawanna, P-U!* my sister and I chanted, pinching our noses, rolling the car windows tight against the sulfurous stench. My friends' parents worked at the mills, at the car plants. When those shut down, in some instances, their sons worked for environmental monitoring companies, testing the abandoned sites for leaching toxins. We came of age an hour's drive from Love Canal, downwind of Three Mile Island, on the heels of *Silent Spring*. The Cold War and fear of nuclear attack—my mind came of age to those nightmare-makers.

My body came of age working the vineyards snaking across Lake Erie's fertile floodplain. Concords grown for juice and jam. In high school I was trimming the leafless vines over spring break; combing the heavy, flyaway new growth bare armed in the heat of summer; harvesting rows too narrow to accommodate mechanical picking machines in September. The grapes were heavily treated with chemicals, something that never crossed my mind. Walking home from school, it was a rite of spring, like bounding, excessive light in April in Alaska: the sick-sweet antifreeze stench hovering in the air after the sprayers had crawled up and down the rows of grapes across the street from my childhood home, the smog-haze that hung in the air, penetrating into our house. I ate, drank, breathed, and practically bathed in grapes dusted with chemicals like Alar, a plant growth regulator banned in 1989 and labeled by the Environmental Protection Agency as a known human carcinogen. Chemically sprayed fruit was a given in my childhood; the only time I heard the word *organic* was in chemistry class. After a two-year 1989 peer-reviewed study, the National Resources Defense Council reported that, via food, "the average preschooler's exposure [to chemicals like Alar] was estimated to result in a cancer risk 240 times higher than the risk considered acceptable . . . following a full lifetime exposure."

I think about that adolescent body that was mine, working the harvest at the Burt farm, just across the horse pasture from our backyard, snipping grape clusters with bare hands, eating grapes until my mouth grew raw. It's easy to romanticize those memories: the smell of ripe grapes rising off the fields in the early September heat, the sweet jelly of flesh the color of cucumber sharpened by the astringency of the skin, the farm lunches breaking up our work days at the Stebbins' big dining room table with a group of sweaty teens, the rituals of picking and preserving fruit with my mother, of walking down the street to buy fresh eggs from the Burts or homemade Italian sausage from the De-Pasquales, or vegetables from the Grizantis' farm stand. I ate with abandon my mother's grape pie, drank her grape juice, slathered her preserves on black Latvian bread. My mother put by jars and jars as well as bags and bags of preserves each year, filling our freezer and the shelves in a dark corner of our basement. Every couple weeks we packed our baskets for another excursion to a U-pick farm, none of them organic or no-spray: cherries, blueberries, peaches, apples. My father sprayed our own orchard and sprinkled chemicals on the vegetable garden. I ate his fruit straight off the branch, the slight pesticide essence woven in with that of plum, pear, and apple. On Fridays, being Catholic, my family ate fish caught in Lake Erie. My body came of age nourished by western New York's soil and water. I ate the place, I breathed it in. It became my body.

In the late winter of 2010, just before I turned forty-six, I crisscrossed that childhood landscape in a rental car. Looking back now, it seems that I carried cancer as an invisible companion occupying the passenger seat, upon which I, oblivious, carelessly tossed mix CDs, coffee cups, empty water bottles, cell phone, bags of trail mix, toll tickets. It was March, and I was driving along the eastern curve of Lake Erie, north across the Peace Bridge to Canada to visit an aunt with pancreatic cancer, west into Ohio to visit my stepson at his college in Gambier and my brother in Mineral Ridge, east again to stay with childhood friends still living near Silver Creek. It was my first time back since my aging parents had moved out of our childhood home to an assisted living facility closer to my sister, who was then on Cape Cod.

As I drove, the landscape triggered an ache of recognition in my chest. The scenery was more familiar than my own eyes in the rearview mirror, more real than my own body on the car seat: grizzle of bare trees and sinuous leafless vineyards and Baltic fields of corn stubble and over all of it, a gusty wind out of a coarse-grained sky. That landscape was mine in a wholly different way than the landscape of Alaska I'd chosen as home, where I'd hightailed myself after college. I'd learned the western New York landscape young by touch and sound. I'd learned it planting potatoes in my parents' garden, learned it as soil embedded under my nails and stained my ankles. I'd learned it scooping up glass jars of minnows as I waded for hours in the creek a half mile from our house, the acrid fish stink clinging to my wet clothes and hands. I'd learned it digging for antique bottles with my friend Elise in the walls of the gorge the creek had carved over eons, learned it troweling up wildflowers with my mother among the discarded washing machines and dumped tires in the woods of the creek bottom. As a young adult I'd learned it backpacking down the creek with my boyfriend, chewing sassafras growing at the ends of grape rows with my fellow farm laborers, ice skating the creek in winter with my girlfriend, skinny-dipping in Lake Erie the night I saw my first red aurora and lost my virginity. I'd learned it with my mind in college, working as a naturalist, studying biology, learning to identify the trees, ferns, and wildflowers by name, spore pattern, flower form. I'd learned the birds by sound, the fish by fin placement, the insects by body type. And I'd learned the landscape again, middle-aged, in another place, Latvia, my parents' birthplace. The landscape of my youth, I discovered when I traveled there in my forties, was an echo of the landscape of theirs.

The dark songs on the mix CD my brother Andy had given me fit the scenes I drove past, the small eroding towns, the Howard Johnsons along the thruway, the vehicle-struck deer laid out on the road shoulder, the messy second-growth woods between fallow fields, the windward-leaning barns with their fading painted-on Mail Pouch Tobacco ads. Silver Creek, and many towns like it, had actually lost population—and jobs—since I'd left, due to the collapse of the steel industry.

I imagine cancer sitting quietly, staring out the window, humming. The actual cancer, unbeknownst to me, I carried in my right breast and in the lymph nodes under my arm. I can't say I was utterly oblivious to its presence. Cancer had tried to announce itself a few months before, first as an ache in my breast, which I'd attributed to strenuous yoga. But the ache had come and gone and come and gone again. One January morning, lying in bed next to my sleeping husband, I'd pushed my fingers deep into my breast, determined to find the source of the ache. There. A hardness, a wrongness, a solidness within softness. I'd shaken Craig awake. *I found a lump in my breast*, I told him as I straddled him and leaned toward him and told him to feel for it. He'd reached up and pressed and groggily said, *No, it just feels like your breast.* The next day, I'd googled the symptom, read that breast cancer rarely presents as pain.

So I'd pushed the wrongness down, deeper into my body. Besides, there is no breast cancer and very little cancer at all in my family, though I must admit, beyond my grandparents, my genealogy recedes into a fog-bank of war and toil, obscured in preliterate Latvia, where my ancestors tilled land as serfs to German overlords and likely died early. Until the early twentieth century, culture and history were completely embodied for my ancestors, not written down: folk dance, needlecraft, riddles, songs, tales, weavings. Religion for my ancestors arose out of nature, gods of sun and thunder. Stories were handed down mouth to ear, and cancer stories never reached my ears. Likely people didn't give voice to such private travails, probably they don't even today.

Genetic testing would eventually reveal one piece of my ancestral story. I didn't carry any known mutations on the inherited breast cancer genes known as BRCA, but I did carry a mutation on the one known as P53, the tumor suppressor gene. It had been turned off by some in-sult somewhere down the line, or perhaps by a random genetic mutation, what recent studies suggest is the trigger for much cancer. The mutation shut off my immune system's ability to fight breast cancer. It was just bad fucking luck—genetics meets life history. My oncologist would later say as much. *We live in a poisoned world. Some people have the genetics to handle it, some don't, that's my sense of it.* Yet despite his statement, the data linking specific environmental toxins unequivocally to breast can-cer is sparse, since testing chemicals on human subjects is unacceptable. Nevertheless, people with cancer, like me, can't help but ask why, can't help but attempt to trace it back to something, to create an origin story. Why me—a nonsmoker, nondrinker, slender, athletic, wilderness lover who (now) eats only organic?

Slowly, though, some data about breast cancer and the environment has begun to emerge. In 2014 the Silent Spring Institute released results of a study that cited gasoline, diesel, and chemicals formed by burning gas among the largest sources of breast carcinogens in the environment. Other chemicals named in the study include organic solvents, flame retardants, and styrene, found in tobacco smoke and Styrofoam. Pesticides, carried in our bodies by most of us in the United States, increase our exposure to xenoestrogens (estrogen mimics) disrupting the endocrine system, basically feeding the processes turning breast cells cancerous. In 2008 a study by the Public Health Institute found that exposure to DDT in girls before mid-adolescence resulted in a fivefold increase in breast cancer risk.

Who could say what, ultimately, seeded the cancer growing in my breast? One too many strawberries, wolfed down unwashed, picking pint after pint beside my mother in the farm field down the road? One too many dollops of grape or gooseberry or blueberry or cherry or strawberry jam? One too many whiffs of pesticide wafting off the vineyards, breathed on my walks home from school? One too many inhalations of my father's cigarette smoke, trapped in its cloud in the family car? One too many dunks in a lake tainted by DDT, PCBs, and heavy metals? One too many shots of tequila in college? One too many pots of Kraft macaroni and cheese? One too many oil changes on my research boat as a grad student in Alaska, not wearing gloves or a respirator? One too many coats of toxic bottom paint slathered on the research boat hull, dribbled on my skin (again no gloves or respirator)? One too many sticks of sugarless gum? One too many smears of antiperspirant? (Those two would be dismissed outright by my oncologist, the others countered with, "It was nothing you did; it was not your fault.") I was forty-five on that drive, already postmenopausal. Still wearing low-cut jeans that pinched my hip bones, still thinking I might one day train for a marathon, still running five miles a day with iPod earbuds pumping music into my head and glands pumping adrenaline into my legs, but how can I say this: disassociated from my body as flesh, which is vulnerable, which is mortal. Disassociated from my body as a repository for my natural history, and the unnatural history of my birthplace. No health insurance, no primary care doctor, some vague and silly plan to head to India or Thailand if I came down with cancer. Twenty-plus years into a life in wild Alaska, obsessive about the purity of what I ate and drank. Yet I was a body passed through four decades of toxic exposure and two environmental disasters close to the places I call home: the 1979 Three Mile Island nuclear accident 250 miles from Silver Creek, and ten years later, the Exxon Valdez Oil Spill in Prince William Sound, where by then I was studying orcas, living a life I could never have foreseen back in Silver

Creek, a girl sliding along the algae-covered bottom of the creek in bare feet, holding her collecting jar.

There are many ways of not knowing, not seeing, and there are equally many ways of knowing, of coming to know deep in your body, embodying knowledge the way my ancestors embodied culture, the way the earth embodies language and spiritual belief and insult. Or maybe what I want to say is that it takes many ways of knowing to overcome your brain's many refusals, to admit you know a thing like cancer resides—is seizing control—inside your body. (To admit, as a culture, that our acts can set a river on fire, kill a lake, poison our food supply, mutate our genes, change the weather.) And then, even if you can admit it for a second, you return to not knowing, and it takes many more ways of knowing after that to incorporate, to accept such frightening truths, and even more ways to act. For the body (for the earth) to whisper it into your own ear, and for you to hear it, to understand the language—how likely is it, without one more hurricane, one more flood, one more failed crop, one more childhood—cancer? So much easier to ignore the fact that body and earth mirror one another.

That January morning my fingers had dug into my breast and found a peach pit, a cobble, a tiger's eye. My mind had dropped like a cement block down into my body when my fingers made contact, and I'd known, instantly but momentarily, bodily with all of me, flesh and brain, what it was. Malignancy. Death encapsulated in my flesh, arising from my own mutated cells. My fingertips had known it and told my brain. My brain had known it and had fallen into my stomach. My stomach had known it and told my mouth. My mouth had whispered it into my ear. It was then only an inch away from my brain. All the knowing had happened in less than a second. And then I'd risen back out of my body and into my head, and said to myself, "No, you are paranoid. It is nothing. No, there is no breast cancer in your family. No. This is not your story."

I became stranded then, in that memory of knowing. I was as alone as I'd ever been in my life, as I'd ever be, after that. Alone in and with my body and its mad, ever-dividing secret. On the road trip, at my childhood friends' house, I swiped fog off the bathroom mirror and stared at my breast, towel at my feet while the shower ran behind me. Now I saw it. My breast deformed by a mound above my nipple. It's astounding how you can inhabit a body and not look at it for months at a time. You can judge your body, evaluate, compare, critique, withhold from or indulge your body but fail to see it. In three months, the unspeakable silent cancer within me had grown from an invisible aching thing to a buried lump to a visible swelling. I had no words for this, though a pathology report would attach to the rapid growth a series of numbers that added up to nine on a scale of one to ten and translated into the adjective "aggressive." But that was yet to come. In the now of myself beholding my misshapen breast in the bathroom mirror before it fogged up again, in the sensation of falling into knowing, it was a secret between my body and me. It was the most intimate with my body I'd ever been. My body was suddenly speaking for itself, and I was, for once, listening. I knew I would not tell my friends, in whose mirror I was looking. I would not tell my husband. Not yet. I couldn't bear to make it real by translating my inner, wordless knowing into words and delivering those words to another person to share with me. I would not tell my sister, who is a doctor, until I saw her in a few weeks' time at the end of my road trip. I would drive my knowing back down, out of reach of consciousness, as I steered my car across New York State's southern tier. I would keep living a story already over. That's what I mean by alone.

Another way of saying: I was, at forty-five, no longer a child. In that moment, I inhabited not a story, but a body, all the way in.

I have told this story now I don't know how many times, and each time, it is a different story. Perhaps each time it's a bit more true. Perhaps each time it's a bit more suspect, a bit more spun, a bit more of an imaginative act, a narrative invention. I would soon tell a version of the story to my sister. I would soon tell pieces of it to a breast specialist. I would tell it to a social worker, a therapist, family, friends. Which story would be most authentic? "Out of narrative truths a sense of coherence can be restored," writes sociologist Arthur A. Frank, in his classic study *The Wounded Storyteller: Body, Illness, and Ethics.* Before coherence, though, there is only the body. There is only the earth. Perhaps the most authentic things are wordless (me standing before the bathroom mirror; that mute, eutrophic eye forming each summer in the middle of Lake Erie), when we're storyless even to ourselves.

I was, that spring, a body plagued by a weird and discomfiting rattle, which a mind tried to ignore. I was a head attached to a body eating handfuls of trail mix, detritus of peanut skins sprinkled all over my lap. I was a body with a pair of forty-five-year-old breasts, one of them cancerous. Writes Frank, "The temporarily broken-down body becomes 'it' to be cured. Thus the self is dissociated from the body. . . . The body is a kind of car driven around by the person inside." My body wasn't yet an "it" to be cured—that was coming—but an "it" to be silenced.

Even when I could no longer deny cancer's existence in my body, I would refuse to call it mine. *The* cancer, I would insist. *The cancer thing*, I would say about the eight months of devastating treatment to come, to friends' perplexed looks. I would abide by the general article, not the specific, possessive pronoun. I'm a writer, a teacher of writing, but I'm also a biologist; I should have known better. The cancer was/is mine. My cancer. No one else's. It was mine not by choice, but in the way western New York was mine, rooted; my origins and its origins were one and the same.

You can say you've found your true home in another landscape, but you can never leave your birthplace behind. I'd headed straight to Alaska out of college to escape the dull, violent horizon of Lake Erie, the insults to the earth embodied there. I'd headed toward a northern horizon, one I'd imagined as untainted, wild. The first time I'd seen Prince William Sound, I'd known with all of me that I was home. But I'd carried my childhood place inside me all that time. And when I returned to that childhood place in the spring of 2010, the inside space where I held it throbbed in acknowledgment. *I am yours, you are mine.* I am claimed by, it turns out, a landscape not only of abuse but endurance: scruffy forests overtaking abandoned farmland; a once-dead lake system still supporting salmon and trout; towns once fueled by long-ago mothballed steel plants and car factories half resurrected with hair and tattoo salons, army-navy stores, 7-Elevens, Subways, pizza parlors, grungy delis; a grape-growing industry diversified from juice and jam to wine. An endurance of small farms, farm stands, greenhouses, some of them even organic today.

Now I study the photographs I took on the road trip, searching for some hidden knowledge on my face, the face of the person who listened for days to dark songs as she drove. I look for it behind my various masks, the shit-eating grin in the photo taken in my stepson's dorm suite when I posed as if playing beer pong with his girlfriend. The demure smile on my Latvian face in the photo in which I'm standing beside my aunt, arm protectively around her shoulder. I tower over her in the photo in my black pea coat. Two women with cancer, one of them diagnosed, treated, bearing up, the other in denial, unwilling to stare again into a full-length mirror. I look like a good niece. I look like a good stepmother. I search for knowledge also in the unphotographed moment when I parked behind the school bus garage in my hometown and walked into the forest I'd helped my father plant when I was a child—a thousand seedlings he'd obtained from the Forest Service. My heart sank, noticing the rubbish on the ground, the empty bottles and trash, the sick state of untrimmed, unthinned spruce trees. I made my way to the woods' edge and covertly photographed the back of the house where strangers now lived.

I stood there holding the camera, unable to believe completely that my parents no longer moved behind those windows. How could it be my father wouldn't emerge onto the back deck to fill the bird feeders? How could it be my mother wasn't knitting in her blue chair in the living room? How could it be I was a trespasser, a stranger, lurking in the forest we'd planted together? How could it be no one tended the orchard, the garden, the bees?

I only see it now, how I stood there in the memory of the house that had been my body, which I'd taken for granted all of my life. From this vantage, that body seems to belong to somebody else, just as the ranch house did. I stood inside the house that was my body, which turned out to have its own will, its own narrative to enact. A tumor had taken root within me, from within me, perhaps as a result of my body's encounter with that very landscape, that very backyard—lake water tainted with DDT, pesticide sprayed on vineyard or U-pick strawberry field or all over my father's apple trees by his own hand. Soon, my body would be occupied, colonized, described, narrated by surgeons, radiologists, phlebotomists, infusion nurses, technicians, doctors, from without. There would be medical charts relating a story of my body I would never read. There would be pathology reports relating a story of my body I would read again and again, searching for omens. My body and its secrets would be breached. I stand now in the memory of a moment lived in ambivalent relation to my body and to the earth out of which it came, when I still thought I owned my future, chose my landscape, and indulged in the idea that I had time to figure out my next move, what I wanted to be, what my life could mean.

How strange that cancer, which often feels like an invader, a colonizer, comes not from without. Cancer is the body. Like Hurricane Katrina, like Hurricane Sandy, like floods in Texas, like drought in California, like zero snowpack in the Olympic Mountains last winter, it is not without external cause—the burning of carbon to fuel our lives. Yet these things we call natural disasters are exactly that: natural. They are natural earthly responses—just as cancer is a bodily response—to grave insult, or to the process of random mutation, by which all species adapt and evolve. How strange that a cancer story is a story of earth, of being a creature on earth—this particular, damaged earth, at this time—a thing of nature, responding to natural laws, like any wild being, be it river or sparrow or cloud. How strange to occupy a mortal body for what is, in the end, a very short time, in total denial of death.

In her face, I see it, that me in the photo not taken that day, death—simply another force of nature—swooping in for a pass, hurtling down from a long way up, wide wings casting a javelin shadow across the tops of the trees above her. In the forest that was once her father's, in the landscape she left that never left her, in the body that was once mine, and always the earth's.

In the Lightless Calm Deep

Leave the door open for the unknown, the door into the dark. That's where the most important things come from, where you yourself came from, and where you will go.

—Rebecca Solnit

I LIE ON MY BACK on my sister Mara's couch and lift my shirt, lift my bra. The rooms around us are dark, except for undercabinet lights illuminating the kitchen counters. Mara's husband, her three young children, are upstairs asleep. The golden retriever is asleep on the other end of the couch. I can't put it off any longer. It's 2:00 a.m. We've been doing what we always do when we spend time together: we've been talking, trying to solve each other's present-day problems, threading them back into our pasts, into our natures. There is no one more intimate with my past and my nature than Mara.

"I'm sure it's nothing. You're forty-five; you have lumpy breasts," she says as she begins slow-circling my breast with her fingers. She's a doctor; she's felt hundreds of breasts. And she's an optimist, at least on the surface level of personality. At least when it comes to those she loves. (I will learn a strange and utterly surprising thing in the months to come: oncologists tend to be optimists too, according to the man who will become mine.)

I watch Mara's eyes. I watch her eyes change expression. I feel her fingers stop. "Is this what you mean? This feels weird, not like a lump so much; it feels like a ridge." She is silent, pressing.

"Stop," I say. "It hurts." I pull down my bra, my shirt. I sit up on the couch. She is already opening her laptop to email her boss, asking for a recommendation for a breast specialist.

"It doesn't feel like any breast cancer lump I've found. It's probably nothing," she says, typing fast. "It could be a fibroadenoma or a benign cyst. Don't worry. We'll get it checked out." She slaps the laptop shut.

In literature, in film, there's a thing called "dramatic irony." It's when a reader sees what's coming for a character, but the character herself doesn't see it coming. It's that moment watching a horror flick when you hiss in the dark theater, "Don't open that door, Goddamn it." This is a scene like that, only the hapless character is me, and I have already walked out the door, I am already lost in the forest, I have already entered the monster's realm. But I deny it to myself; I breathe in my sister's reassurance like a deep drag off a joint. My sister's control of the situation calms me. I go to sleep in the attic guest room reassured that everything will be all right.

I don't know what happens in the room below mine. How my sister climbs into her bed and wakes up her husband, sobbing. How she says, "Eva has a lump in her breast. It's probably cancer."

I look back on this moment from another present tense. It is 2015, and I'm sitting in the aft cabin of our research boat, *Natoa*, at the tiny desk beside our bunk, looking up now and then to stare past rain streaking down the window to the view of the Cordova Harbor. Boat engines throb. The gillnet fleet is getting ready for the first salmon opener next week. Wind shoulders in heavy gusts against the *Natoa*'s side, and she sways and strains against her lines and buoys. In Hinchinbrook Entrance, where my husband, Craig, and I have been working the last week to document orca pods and humpback whales—something we've done each summer for more than thirty years—it's blowing forty knots, a full gale. That place, with its tide rips and currents and ten-mile-wide opening to the Gulf of Alaska, is a maelstrom today. But the orcas we study don't care. They go about their business, echolocating down the outer coast of Montague Island searching for salmon, the newborn calves at their mothers' sides, surfacing among mountainous waves, like any other day. It's easy to forget they spend more than 90 percent of their time below the water's surface, where, diving deep, they find calm. It's easy to forget the lightless, groundless realm is home to them.

Above them, above us, the storm system is massive, its center five hundred miles to the west, over Kodiak Island. This is just its edge. It is forecast to blow like this for four days. On Sunday, when we will head back out to the Entrance to resume our work, I will turn fifty-two. I have traveled five years and a long way from that person I was, the woman asleep in my sister's house on Cape Cod.

I creep up the carpeted stairs and stand over her form, curled up under the down comforter on the foldout couch bed. Beside her on the nightstand is her journal, her pile of books, her collection of stones and talismans from Alaska. An orange cat sleeps against her back. Through the dormer window, I can see the shadow-line of the horizon: Cape Cod Bay in half moonlight. It will be her horizon for a time, but she doesn't know that yet. She has cracked open the window to let in the sound of spring peepers going at it in the marsh and the cool, rank scent of estuary wafts into the room.

I've learned something about self-mercy in the last five years. I reach out my hand to move a strand of hair from her face. I know everything will not be all right. I know some things she doesn't know, can't imagine. I know that she will not return to Alaska in a few days, as planned. I know she will spend eight months sleeping in that attic room, and that sometimes she will be so anemic from chemo that she will have to ascend the final set of stairs on hands and knees. I know that she will miss her field season in Prince William Sound for the first time in twenty years. I know that she will close her heart to Cape Cod, like Odysseus's wife, Penelope, closing her heart to her suitors despite her husband's interminable absence. She will compare Cape Cod unfavorably every day to Alaska. I know that mercy is present for her in this place, in human form but more importantly in the earth, in the wildness that remains on the cape, just as mercy was present for her in the abused, enduring landscape of her youth. In the dunes amid the juniper bushes and beach plums, on Wing Island, in the marshlands, in the ponds, in the scruffy, low pine woods infested with Lyme ticks, in the white cedar swamp, mercy will be present, it will enter her, though she will resist it. It will become a part of her. I know I will have to leave her like this, fully aware of how she'll become lost in her anguish, in her self-pity and rage, in her displacement, in the darkness, finding her way toward the solace of every wild and wild-ish place as she finds her way home. Perhaps, like those orcas in the stormy entrance, she is already submerged in that lightless calm deep, and there, some part of her will stay below the chaos. Perhaps more than what happens on the surface—the scarring, the damage, the sickness, the endurance—what will change her most will happen down there.

I know this is the end of the world as she's known it. I know it is the beginning of the world as I know it now—contingent, damaged, yet beautiful and alive. There is no map to the place where we are going. We will be lost for a good, long time.

Nipple Unremarkable

As I trudge around my sister's Cape Cod lawn in the dark, trying to walk off chemo's nausea and reflux, trying to breathe past the spike in my throat, I recite in my head a mantra of names from my home in Alaska, thousands of miles away: Iktua Bay, Squire Island, Point Helen, Lucky Bay, Green Island, Long Channel, Dangerous Passage, Danger Island. But names alone can't displace the power of this new hot, humid place where I'm being treated for breast cancer. The names are drowned out by the belling decibels of spring peepers in the swamps across the road, by the voices of late-night dog walkers, by the smears of tires on the wet asphalt of Route 6A. More than that, the names can't displace a new language of strange, dense words lapping their colorless syllables into my ear. Nor the new sensations: my body, sliced, stitched, bandaged, pierced, infused, irradiated, pricked, transfused, staged, anesthetized. Chemo-brained, nerve-numbed, de-marrowed, yellowed. Though deflowered and defoliated, nonetheless pinked. Pinned, beribboned. In breast cancer chat rooms you find women at all hours asking advice about side effects of treatment, answering, talk-story-ing, worse-case-scenario-ing, signing off, not with their given names, but with their diagnoses, a string of numerals, abbreviations: cancer slang like this:

peace and love, apple – aka, Mary Magdalen
Diagnosis: 4/10/2008, IDC, 5 cm, Stage 4, Grade 3, 4/9 nodes, mets,
ER+, HER2+

Years ago, when I moved into my first Alaskan cabin—uneasy during the eighteen-hour nights, nervous in the woods alone with a door that wouldn't lock and my nearest neighbor a persistent guy who didn't own a car, just a snowmachine—I chose an alias for my phone book listing. I renamed myself Ivanna Ivins, thinking it would somehow keep me safe. One night the neighbor guy came knocking at my door anyway. Only the barking dog drove him away.

Who are you now, and are you safe, I ask my new self, my new alias: IDC, 2.5 cm, Stage 2A, Grade 3, 4/14 nodes, HER2-, ER/PR++?

Close your eyes, slow your breathing. Imagine a sheet of paper on a picnic table, held in place by a magnifying glass. Walk to the picnic table. Sit down, pick up the paper, try to decipher a language brute and unfamiliar: Stitch short = superior, long = lateral. A right breast mastectomy without an axillary tail measures 18.0 x 17.0 x 5.0 cm. It weighs 339 grams. The skin is unremarkable. The areola measures 3 x 3 cm and the nipple measures 1.5 x 1.3 cm and is grossly unremarkable. Like seeds, spit the words out of your mouth.

Someone turns me on to yet another language, meditation CDs for cancer patients—one for surgery, another for chemo, another for radiation, another for fear. A woman named Belleruth's voice in my ear each night, intoning: *Imagine a place where you feel safe . . .*

I meditate upon it—no, I study it. No. I deconstruct. I read it again and again, the pathology report, ciphering out clues, searching for what I might have missed. Only after months do my eyes land on those words and stick: grossly unremarkable.

Close your eyes. Breathe. Count backward from ten. Imagine a text, a page torn from a book, lying on a picnic table in Nickerson State Park, in the sun. Ninety-five degrees in the shade of unfamiliar trees, pines and scruffy oaks. Blue jays. Paint blistered off the wood of the table. A few crumbs. Sand grains. Burn ring from a magnifying glass on the page. A sudden, hot gust lifts it up, carries it away, into the woods. Does someone chase after it? Does it land facedown in Cliff Pond? Whose face appears reflected beside it? A face devoid of frame, lashes, brows? Is that really you? Is that me?

Other phrases, like "early stage" I roll around in my mouth with pleasing others: "curative," "survival." They taste better, but still can't erase the bitterness. Early maybe, but still she's "invasive," she's aggressive, she's only stage 2, but not 1. Not 0, like some of those luckies chatting on Breastcancer.doc, first names all DCIS. The sisters in situ. IDC, in contrast, is invasive: she trespasses, colonizes. Invasive Ductal Carcinoma. The most common, unremarkable form of the disease. No. That is not my name.

Treatment as cookbook recipe: one part surgery, two parts chemotherapy, one part radiation, five parts hormone therapy. Layer in naturopathic medicine, spiritual healing.

On the ultrasound image the tumor is gray, barely distinguishable from the surrounding normal, fibrous tissue, a nodule sprouting tendrils. In the pathology report, it's described as a 2 cm spiculated mass. My mind reaches past the disease lingo to a place I love (*imagine a place where you feel safe*), Prince William Sound, Alaska. I imagine that place for metaphor, for ideas of the familiar made strange; the strange, familiar; the dangerous, safe. Prince William Sound, a roadless archipelago where my husband and I have studied killer whales each summer for the last twenty-four years, is a rainforest. It is cool, even when the sun shines. In late summer, rain falls nearly every day. Clouds felt together, descend and erase the mountains. Cloud-skeins catch on the tips of spruce and hemlock. Storms are waterfall-makers. The saturated, mossy earth can't hold all the moisture falling from the clouds, and it plunges down the granite cliffsides and rills, white with oxygen, into the sea. Tiny coves where we anchor our boat turn viscous and green, and from a kayak, I can dip my cup into the freshwater lens and drink ions of alpine tundra, avalanche slope, muskeg, forest duff. Lion's mane jellyfish, as if called by the sound of rushing water to a death fugue, aggregate near stream outfalls and die en masse. Their red-orange bodies whiten. Ghostlike, they drift and disintegrate, their tentacles dragging along the rocky bottom, tangling in eelgrass.

The tumor's tendrils twine, creep toward the lymph node under my arm. After surgery, some pathologist typed out words devoid of metaphoric possibility, words I read again and again, uncomprehending. The ghost-jellies of the sound eventually dissolve in the sea, are reabsorbed. The ghost-jelly in my breast, and the breast itself, and that grossly unremarkable nipple, are who-knows-where. And I am who-knows-where. And so I meditate. In the lingo, I visualize.

Imagine a safe, loved place. Drag your kayak up the beach of Squire Island and tie it to a log. Slog through the muskeg meadow behind the pond where wild irises grow and your boots sink into sphagnum and mud. Enter the forest and climb the steep bank, pulling yourself up by blueberry branches to the big hemlock. Over twenty years you've wept into its lichen-encrusted bark, nails dug into moss at its base, as gales hissed through the branches high above. Sit with your back against the trunk. Close your eyes. Listen to the hermit thrushes and fish crows. Hear waves slapping the beach below. Sense someone there. Open your eyes and see arriving a black bear. Put your hand to the flank of the bear. Breathe in the musty stench of skunk cabbage, den, and fawn. Imagine her fierceness as cure, how it passes into you through your palm and travels up your right arm to the scar.

A few days before my surgery, I hike to a beach called Crow's Pasture with my new friend Lauren. A trail through a forest of stunted pitch pine, scrub oak, and tick-infested brush leads to the dunes. Lauren's nine years' post (I don't know her diagnostic name, I've never asked), what they call, in the jargon of the disease, a "survivor." This is her place, the way Prince William Sound is mine. Today, the air cool, the flat gray sky threatening rain, the dunes are deserted. Far out on the tide-exposed flats, figures of clam diggers bend and straighten. I can't get used to this idea of horizon, sea and sky clamped to each other along an unbroken line, no mountains to intervene.

First, Lauren and I find a knife in the sand, a knife with a red plastic handle and a retractable blade, a fisherman's knife. And a few steps away, three square plastic dice. Instead of odds, these dice spell out "sly." Around a bend of beach, we find the corpse of a common dolphin. Finally, we find a tree covered with nodules. Tumor-tree, we call it, and I wonder what it means for us, this constellation of signs. Are they omens? Hopeful or not? Who gets to wield the knife?

Imagine a place you love. The innermost sanctum of that place. Wait for the tide to rise, to drown the waterfall pouring out of the hidden lagoon. Kayak up the channel, into the lagoon, pushing against the water's flow, watching eelgrass streaming in the opposite direction. Nose your kayak up to the gravelly bank of a streambed littered with bleached, eyeless, spawned-out salmon bodies. Kneel over the fresh carcass of a coho salmon, a red-handled knife in your hand. Beside you a black bear teaches you how to eat again, how to replace your body, cell for cell. Start with the head, he says. Tear away operculum, gill. Start with the brain. The seat of language.

Chemo leaves me bald and yellow-nailed, like a punk rocker or a chronic smoker. Is that because Cytoxan is derived from mustard gas? A thin layer of my face, Dijon brown, rubs off in the shower. Skin so dry, I go through a bottle of vitamin E oil in a week. Months later, I stand in front of a mirror, my fingers tracing my skin's new leaves, my head's white, infantile fluff.

On a meditation CD, Belleruth, with her soothsayer's voice, instructs me to visualize in my body an army of fierce and hungry white cells and I, their commander. I close my eyes and hear, like a hive of bees, beneath the sluice of blood pulsing in my ears, a thrumming horde in my bone marrow. I command. But the fierceness dies within me, no match to my fear of cancer. So I imagine predators. I imagine killer whales, their echolocation so precise they can single out one fat-rich king salmon from a school of ten thousand leaner pink salmon. Killer whales swimming through my circulatory system, echolocating down the channels of lymph and blood, searching for the errant cells, the mutant traces, ushering them out. Along with the attendant language. No longer syllables or words, but cancer's shattered alphabet, driven out of my mouth by whales whose Latin name means "from death's realm."

Despite the pink language of hope, the green language of survival, the white language of statistics and stages, one red word overshadows every other. On mudflats on Cape Cod, and in Prince William Sound, a crab, a sidewise-scuttling creature, is comical, tentative, quick to retreat under a rock or frond. This is no such animal. Cancer is sly, a red-handled knife. Three dice tossed in the sand, spelling out its true name. Sly. In the gray language of fear.

Imagine a glacier-fed stream pouring down from the mountain into the tidal lagoon. Amid rocks and blue-black piles of bear scat, salmon carcasses litter the grass, their faces chewed off by river otters and bears, their eyes gouged out by gulls. Get on your knees and sip the water from the stream like a deer. Drink until your jaws ache, until the chemo's heat in your body cools. Then lie face down. Place your face on a swath of sea paper—amalgam of algae, eelgrass, and kelp—stretched between grass blades, studded with tiny snails. Breathe in the smell of salt and decay and damp stones. Clutch grass in your fists. Know you could die right here, today, and it would be okay.

Red again. The rash begins along the rib bone below the scar, spreads up to my neck, ruby regalia, wild fire. Every morning, I drape a washcloth soaked in ice water across the burn before stepping into the shower. Every afternoon I walk through the three-inch-thick door with its radiation hazard sign to lie on my back on a cold slab, a warmed blanket over my body, except for my exposed right chest. I'm held in place by a plastic form, my arms overhead, hands gripping a metal bar, feet gently bound with a strap while the technicians measure me with a plastic ruler and call out numbers – *99 and 1.5–2.2 deep with MLC.* As the table rises and shifts, laser lights draw red lines across my chest and on the walls. Then the technicians say "We'll be right back," flick on the overhead fluorescent lights, and leave me alone. Me and my shadow, a depthless eye tilted above my left shoulder. I count breaths as the machine clicks and buzzes. Shouldn't this sting? Tingle? I keep my eyes closed. But I feel nothing. *Remember,* I tell myself, *to breathe. Imagine looking into a deer's eyes. Imagine the cool light of the moon.*

Halfway through radiation, Craig and I take our bikes on the ferry to Nantucket for a weekend. It is October now. Biking around the island one morning, I pedal hard against a spiked autumn wind, the paved trail taking us mile by mile away from Nantucket town with its cobblestone lanes and high-end shops and whaling captains' mansions into the island's heart, a rolling landscape of low plants frost-burned to russets. It reminds me of alpine tundra. A month out from chemo, my red blood count hasn't quite bounced back. My calf muscles ache, trying to keep up with Craig, who gradually pulls ahead of me. I can almost believe, standing up to pedal, it will come back to me—my body as it was.

And then I find a dead deer beside the path. She lies on her side, her black liquid eye looking past my shoulder at the pale blue sky, at a translucent wedge of moon. I kneel by her side and touch her forehead and her cheek, her hard flank. Surreptitiously, I slip my hand in my pocket and feel for my cell phone. I photograph her, I don't know why, and feel strangely ashamed. Then I bike fast to catch up to Craig, to turn him around, to show him the deer, not its morbidity—its beauty. I don't show him the secret photograph I keep.

The machine rotates. Its metal teeth shift expressions. After the last zap, the machine emits a strange fluttery sound, like frozen lashes falling on crusty snow. It clicks off, the eye closes. I lower my arms.

Imagine first snow falling on the body of the deer, melting in the pool of its skyward-facing eye. Imagine yourself held inside that water, blessedly cool, a secret in your pocket.

Back at the beginning, waiting for surgery, I grew, for the first time in my life, tender toward my breast. At night, I placed my left hand on the lump and my right hand on my heart and imagined compassion flowing from right to left, from heart to breast. I wept for it. By day, I ate kale, turmeric, garlic, flax oil. During hot yoga, my hands slid across my yoga mat; my sweat smelled toxic. *Imagine a dolphin guiding the cancer out of your body, back to source,* the hypnotic voice of Belleruth said through my iPod earbud each morning. *Be gone, be gone,* chanted the spiritual healers. I felt empowered. But as the weeks wore on, the terror grew beyond tenderness and effort. I'm done, I thought, every time I looked in the mirror after a shower at the swollen dome above my nipple. Bring on the surgeon. Bring on the red-handled knife. Take this pound of flesh. When I awoke from anesthesia and looked into the surgeon's eyes, I didn't ask, "Was it in the lymph nodes?" I said, "Thank God it's out; thank God it's over." I didn't ask, "Where is it now, my breast?" In the hospital room, I stared down at the gown where it lay flat across the bandage. No pain. No sensation. The bliss of disappearance.

Only later, when I read the pathology report, when I read those words "nipple grossly unremarkable" did I wonder who'd dissected it. I wondered where he or she had taken the remains. I mourned the breast then, its fate. I heard later about a woman who asked for her breast, and got it, and in a ceremony, placed it at the bottom of a deep hole into which her friends planted an apple tree. That unbearable Cape Cod summer, when I stood in the outdoor shower and stared at myself in the mirror and ran my fingers along the scar, I thought about that breast, that nipple. What place did they take it to, that mound of caressed, abused, longed for, hidden, and rejected flesh? The hospital incinerator? A freezer? A dumpster? That breast with all its stories and longing. Marked. Remarked upon. Unremarkable. Unable to remark. Who-knows-where is as good as nowhere. I would like to have taken it to that safe, loved place.

Then I realized I could. And so I do.

Imagine a place so powerful you refuse to utter its name, its latitude or longitude. You call it by another name now, the center of the labyrinth, where the essence of Prince William Sound rises up as mist from the surface of the tidal lagoon, spills from the waterfall as clots of foam, mingles with sea grass to form paper, enters your body as breath. A place that knows your true name. The place where, once, you died, and it was okay. Kayak to the waterfall, where the jellyfish and salmon steady themselves in the current. From your pocket, pull out the breast. Put your lips to the nipple. Hold it in your palm as you submerge your hand in the water. Let it go. Watch it turn green as it drops to the bottom and disappears beneath the jellyfish and salmon.

Re-Covering the Body

And where is the safest place when that place must be someplace other than in the body?

—Claudia Rankine

And where is that safest place when you learn both body and terrain can be breached and harmed? When language, that other safest place, can fail? The state of emergency is also always a state of emergence.

—Homi Bhabha

THE BODY'S QUESTIONS, LIKE LANGUAGES, originate in the earth; they return to the earth. They are before/under/beyond language, before/under/beyond any story we might tell ourselves or tell others—our myths. The stories we tell are our attempts at answers. "We tell ourselves stories in order to live," Joan Didion famously wrote. But sometimes the questions we ask are not narrative, not story, but lyric, the realm of poetry, or prayer. We ask ourselves those kinds of questions in order to live with uncertainty.

Arthur Frank calls the dominant illness story in our culture "the restitution narrative." He calls it "illness in the imaginary." He writes, "The restitution story is about remaking the body in an image derived either from its own history before illness or from elsewhere." In cancer center brochures, he writes, you rarely see ill patients. You see patients restored to their former selves, post-treatment. In an article in *Yoga Journal* sent to me by a friend, a yoga teacher with breast cancer was photographed in various yoga poses on her infusion chair, an IV hooked to her arm vein. There was no hint of suffering on her face, no hint of wasting on her toned body. Her discipline, her strength, the images claimed, carried her through to the other side of cancer, bald but otherwise unscathed, perhaps even stronger than before. In environmental science, this story is called "restoration."

After breast cancer treatment, I felt scathed. I felt within me a razed landscape, a nothing where something called a self once lived, and I ran and I hiked and I wrote to restore it, the way a farmer tills bio-char and composted fish carcasses into abused, denuded ground; the way, after a spill, scientists seed hydrocarbon-eating bacteria onto oiled beaches. In the locker room at the fitness club, I hid my scarred body from the other bodies around me. I wore a silicone prosthesis in my bra. I faced a corner when I took off my bra after yoga, wrapped myself in a towel to walk to the shower and back. A friend encouraged me not to hide that way. "It would be good for people to see the reality of breast cancer." But I saw no other obviously one-breasted woman sauntering around naked in the locker room. I didn't feel strong enough to billboard my body that way. I imagined children staring, asking their mothers for explanations. My bra on, I turned from my corner, displaying a restored figure.

I knew from living through an oil spill, the 1989 *Exxon Valdez* disaster in Prince William Sound, that restoration is a myth, and that the illusion of restoration promulgates another kind of damage. Millions of dollars were spent by Exxon to promote the myth of restoration. As with cancer, a battle metaphor was employed after the spill to suggest human triumph over "the accident." Millions of dollars more were spent by agencies to restore salmon habitat, eelgrass beds, sea otter populations, and herring runs in Prince William Sound. Yet the place as it had been could never be resurrected. Even today, twenty-six years later, herring, orcas, and seabirds haven't recovered to former numbers.

The spring after the spill, I sat on a beach log in a cove deep inside Herring Bay. It was a place I'd followed mammal-eating orcas hunting the shorelines for harbor seals. It was a place overrun the summer before by cleanup vessels. It was a place whose rocky shoreline had been blasted with hot water to rid it of visible traces of oil. It was a place where the harbor seals on their haul outs had been coated black with crude, lethargic from breathing its toxic fumes. It was a place where sea otters still dug into intertidal substrate to unearth clams, then ingested the hydrocarbons trapped there.

The bay was quiet that day, enveloped in fog. I was twenty-five years old. I'd just begun my research project when the spill hit. Nothing in my life had prepared me for the scale of loss in the sound. Where I sat, my gumboots were entwined with young beach peas. Toeing around, I uncovered a mat of oil beneath the greenery. It stained the rubber of my boot tip. A stench of asphalt wafted up. I knelt and parted the beach peas to get a closer look. Imbedded in the tarry black mat were thousands of brown flecks: spruce needles dropped from the forest above. And poking up through the oil were new blades of grass.

This is the image not of restoration, but recovery. I don't mean recovery in the sense we think of it, of recovering to a former state from an injury or illness. We are encouraged to leave the painful past behind, to move forward. The future layers—re-covers—the past with our living. Time re-covers the body's wounds with scar tissue. Hair grows back. We re-cover evidence of a mastectomy with new breasts or prostheses. We re-cover baldness with wigs or headscarves. These things hide our losses, but never erase them.

For me, recovery from anything has been the way life pushes up past memory that longs only for its own burial. To bury memory of disaster is to smother both grass and poison, growth and demise. Eventually, the seasons lay more and more grasses down over the mat of oil; time conceals evidence of the damage, but it remains a part of the substrate. You might call it restoration, but you would be wrong. Nothing can recover to a former state, nothing can be restored in the way we unconsciously think of that word. The damaged body, the damaged place, is reformed. In the process, the past is embodied. Covered again, stored. And sometimes it is storied. And hopefully it is remembered.

Never again, we pray, Craig and I, as we watch the tankers come and go out of Hinchinbrook Entrance, even today. Often we watch them while following whales in our boat. Often those whales feed on salmon right in the path of the tankers. Sometimes the captains call us to ask what the hell we're doing in the traffic lane. Now those tankers are escorted by high-tech tugs. Now they are followed out of the iceberg and rock riddled passage by high-tech radar. Now the tankers have double-walled hulls.

Never again, I prayed the winter of my recovery from breast cancer treatment. But cancer, which can be triggered by byproducts of oil, is in many ways like oil. As soon as oil leaves the ground, where it's been held for millions of years, there are no guarantees. As soon as breast cancer forms in the body, no matter how thorough and harsh the treatment, there are no guarantees it won't come back, sometimes in other forms, sometimes years or decades later. The summer of my treatment was the summer of the Deepwater Horizon, the Gulf of Mexico oil spill, two decades after the *Exxon Valdez*. We want progress, forward momentum, but the world spins.

Even though I knew firsthand the myth of restoration, of some linear healing path, I enacted it those months of recovery.

Poet Mark Nepo writes, "In diagnosis, I feared surgery. In surgery, I feared treatment. In treatment, I feared stronger treatment. In recovery, I fear recurrence. No one can avoid this straying, but our health depends on the breath that stops us from straying further. No matter how far we've gone, it is the practice of returning to whatever moment we are living now that restores."

Anatole Broyard, a literary critic who considers his cancer in a book called *Intoxicated by My Illness*, defines "soul loss": "When your soul leaves, the illness rushes in." Broyard writes, "Poetry, for example, might be defined as language writing itself out of a difficult situation."

> soul writing itself out of
> self writing itself out of
> mind writing itself out of
> earth writing itself out of
>
>   terror, loss

Island of Wings: Three Days

On the boat, rocking, anchored in Thumb Cove, I'm sitting at the table in the cabin staring out the window at mountain slopes still buried deep in old, streaked, pocked snow, the remnants of another Alaska winter decaying into forgetfulness. Hanging above avalanche debris, pocket glaciers glow an eerie bubblegum blue. Though the snow below them will be gone in a month, those ancients will persist, a reminder of what's to come, and what's been, all the way back to the Little Ice Age, ten thousand years ago, when they were formed. A loss of glaciers is more than a loss of beauty; it's a loss of geologic memory.

Through the opened window, a north wind blows in old snow's exhalation, which is metallic, sharp, and iodized, a little bitter like the taste of icicles. It's 9:00 p.m., and Craig is already asleep in the bunk. No matter how well we plan ahead, no matter how many years we've done this (twenty-eight for me, thirty-five for Craig), getting from home to the research boat is always an exhausting rush. We pack the car to the gills with gear and food. We move our lives onto the *Natoa* for two weeks: cardboard boxes of dry food, coolers of perishables, duffels of clothes, my satchel of books weighing at least twenty pounds, my oboe, Craig's guitar, cameras, biopsy dart guns, satellite tagging crossbow, recording devices, laptops. We stop halfway from Homer to Seward, a three-and-a-half-hour drive, at the big box grocery store to buy milk, cheese, produce. In Seward, we pull up to the ramp, grab a cart, and wheel loads down to the boat. After the first load, I stay aboard and put away food in drawers and cubbies under seats. Craig hauls the rest of the gear, runs to the hardware store for something or other, and then, everything still in chaos, we untie, push off, and I finish organizing while Craig drives us out of the harbor toward Thumb Cove for the night. We say good-bye to our cell phones, the worldwide web, say hello to the only web that will matter for the next two weeks: the web that we'll enter when we land our first fish, gather our first fistful of salt bush to steam. Always by the time we drop anchor for the night, we're too exhausted to cook, and still tied to the human world, we heat up some boxed soup for dinner.

Breath of life, divine teacher, the chant I'm listening to on my iPod says, *I bow to you again and again.* For me, the breath of life tonight is wind off the snowfields, divine teacher is the mountain range that holds the snows, and the cloud cover that makes them, and the melt rushing down, melt I'll gather in large glass bottles to drink. Along with everything else we leave behind when we leave the harbor, I leave cancer too. Not literally, of course—if it's still in me, I carry it wherever my body goes—but cancer in the abstract, cancer as a mental state. Cancer becomes purely a bodily matter, a matter of scar tissue, or I strive to make it so. Cooped up in the tiny space of the boat, there is little room for cancer as idea, so every morning, I brush its presence out of my brain by looking out the window above our bunk and telling myself, "This is all that matters; this is all there is; there is nothing I can do or think to change a damn thing about cancer." Sometimes I sob a bit, the way a mountain shakes off old snow in a spring avalanche, which we hear often in spring in this cove, the thunder of it shedding, baring rock wall and deeper layers of cold.

I stare out of the window now, listen to the familiar tick of the stove pump, and I'm filled with a sense of being finally home, back on the water after a long absence, returned to our work researching whales, returned to the place I longed for that hot Cape Cod chemo radiation summer when I missed my first field season in twenty-something years because breast cancer came smashing into our lives. Now I've returned with my binoculars and my journal, in which I try to write my soul back into some new way of being—isn't this what's supposed to happen? I mean, you can't just go back to the way it was before. Cancer is supposed to change everything, right? Craig thinks we can go back to how it was before, wants to. But I don't. Every time I look in a mirror after a shower, my altered body reminds me. My right breast is gone. My hair is short and curly. Wouldn't getting cancer be a waste, just some ordinary bump in the road, if not for the chance of the soul getting resurrected, the soul reformed out of new and familiar materials? Dogged by fear, unable to remain present, baffled by mundane mental states and endless strayings from something I'm supposed to call "the path," I've tried to coax out of myself, out of bodily and spiritual damage, a few green shoots, some strand worth following.

Though I love living on this boat, it's hard to leave our house in springtime, to tear myself away from that version of home: the forest all around alive with spring birdsong; the nettle shoots greening up the leaf-littered forest floor, picked with gloves on to steam; the first shoots of sorrel in the garden; the nubs of rhubarb swelling, reddening; the crocuses here and there clustered together as though for warmth. But whenever I get on the boat, it seems I've left useless things behind, come with only the minimal necessities. I stop caring if I wear the same pair of pants day after day, the same sweater. I return to something essential, a kind of salvation, what I am with so much stripped away. I know this sense of well-being I feel here, drinking tea, watching gulls swoop down at salmon fry pimpling the water's surface, is fleeting—this sense of water endlessly moving, of Walt Whitman's cradle endlessly rocking. I scan around the cove with binoculars, looking for a stream pouring down from the snowfields, a stream where I'll kayak tomorrow morning to fill what I jokingly call our "water casks," a term lifted from reading books about Antarctic explorations. I imagine the cup my hand will make dipping water from the stream to taste it (each place I gather water, I swear to Craig, yields a different flavor); I imagine bringing it to my mouth. In the mountains ringing the cove, there are cups the earth has made—a cirque, a valley, a cove. The thing that's held is me, us, time. And part of the ache inside me that feels half like nostalgia and half like secret pleasure comes from the knowledge that it's all fleeting. (The water in my cupped hand leaks out drip by drip no matter how tight I clench my fingers, so I drink fast, slurp it up.)

Speaking of time, can it be true that it's a year and a half since I've been here? That I've lived out one whole year and half of another away from this place? Been given 545 days, scooped each one into my cupped hand, drunk it down? All of these days, embedded inside me now? That

I'm given another, this one with quivery, mercuric water twitching like the hide of a horse? I feel the external things falling away, how I am defined by others, how I measure myself against others, all the meanness, all definitions slipping away. This is mercy, this right-now-awareness-stopped-time-sensation one of my grad students calls "momentness." The thing a poem tries to capture but can't. This is it. And of course it's always present, this mercy, and was a year ago, two, forty-five. There are animals who've died in the deep winter snows I'm looking at, animals buried in avalanches, there are hunted and killed birds, and still, mercy is present in this place. Coming to water is coming into the presence of this mercy. And because I know this feeling of mercy is fleeting, like these old snow-fields, like this moment of calm, I pin it to the page, right here:

2.

It didn't last, no. This is another kind of momentness, the merciless kind. Out in rough water following a small pod of orcas, I'm seasick, and I can't help myself, it reminds me of chemo. Not just the nausea but the trapped feeling. Here, I am trapped by a limited set of sensations, a limited palette of colors (mostly grays), a limited acoustic repertoire (chugging of pistons, groan of engine, clanks of shifting gears, the boat's sway and shudder). Where is the silvery light, the mercy? Mark Nepo writes, "No matter how I lift my heart, my shadow creeps in wait behind, background to my joy." This is fleeting, but in the grip of the unmerciful, that awareness is lost, or is irrelevant. Conclusion: I am NOT enlightened. All around me, the islands we walk on at night speak to it: merciful, merciless life.

3.

I dreamed that cancer came back, Dr. S— told me I had five days left to live, just five, five exactly. At first, I railed, I screamed, clawed, wept, raged. Impossible that I could let life go. But then, as in a dream I had just about a year ago, this strange fog began to creep in, on the inside, a sort of grogginess, a little like anesthesia. And I began to let go. And it was easy. I lay down to die, perhaps the way a moose in deep snow does. It was so natural. This year, a lot of moose died around Homer in the hard, long winter, the deep snows. One day, Craig and I, out skiing, spotted two brown bear juveniles playing with the bones and hide of a moose, throwing them around a creek bottom. They were alive on the snow, in the sunlight, unaware of us, and the moose was over, and yet it was present, a part of the living earth, its surface, like a piece of ordinary detritus that makes up one of artist Sarah Sze's sculptures. Divorced from its moose-story. A player in some other, ongoing history of life on earth, a plaything in the earth's ongoing memoir.

Today, I kayaked to a rocky shoreline, carefully extricated myself from the cockpit, scrambled up into the forest, and followed the trail of river otters through the blueberry thickets. Suspended from branches, all along the trail, were the black-and-white wings of murres, seabirds killed by some predatory bird, probably a peregrine falcon. They looked almost like they'd been impaled on the branches. Or like they'd been carelessly shed, cape-skins thrown over twigs, then abandoned to the rain. The sharp breastbones protruding from matted feathers, marking the place where the spirit of the bird detached and fled.

When I love it out here, it's because in the woods all my fear of dying goes away. It is no mystery, just the facts: these wings were once murres. But that's not so. I look carefully for signs of bears. I do not want to die of cancer; I do not want to be eaten by a bear. How I will die: that knowledge isn't given. That I will die: that knowledge is given, before me right here.

Tonight, in the near darkness, the island of severed wings is alive with the cheeps of nesting storm petrels, who come off the sea only once each year, at night, to burrow into the ground under tree roots or tussocks to lay their eggs. An island of hungry mouths. Bones and feathers litter the burrow entrances. The body, my body, yours, is a similar island. Little deaths, and the urge to live, manic aliveness, bottomless depression, coexisting, feathers, bones, eggs, cheeps. In the body, little deaths asleep, burrowed in the bones, lungs, brain, or liver, and every moment, the body replenishing itself, renewed. William Stafford said, "The darkness around us is deep," but so is the light. The light around me is so damn deep.

I dip my hands into this stream, and all I have is what the stream yields up, what's in this cup of my palm, this sip, these severed wings, that silver light, this moment. Today I followed the stream to its source, a pond in the forest half filled with snow. From its mud-bottom, the water looked nearly black. Half-white and frigid with enormous anvils of snow. Surrounded by forest, by nests and corpses of seabirds, I kneeled down in the mud, filled my hands, and drank it all.

For a World That I Could Love

My house long since lies in rubble. I keep on rebuilding it and reality keeps
tearing it down. Maybe it's better to make peace with the ruins?
                                                        —Anna Kamienska

THE POLISH WRITER ANNA KAMIENSKA kept extensive notebooks
of short entries that read like snippets of conversation with an imaginary
friend, with the divine, with herself, with life. By turns ironic, dark, literary, spiritual, and wry, each seems an attempt to answer some question
only the heart can hear. She lived through World War II and the death
of her husband from cancer in 1967. That trauma transformed her sense
of purpose and defined the spiritual trajectory of the notebooks until
her death in 1986. A poet friend called her "a soul in revolt, a spiritual
quester." A section of her notebooks called "In That Great River" was
published in *Poetry* magazine, and I had that issue with me when I was
diagnosed with breast cancer. I read those entries so many times during
chemotherapy that the pages grew mottled from spilled tea, folded and
bent from being propped open, the spine of the volume cracked. The
magazine came with me to Hawaii, where Craig and I recovered from
our eight-month-long cancer ordeal. Sitting at a desk in our cabin every
morning, I read and reread Kamienska's words the way I once read the
Bible as a child, then the *I Ching* in my twenties. The purpose of her
notebooks, and the purpose of my life those months, could be defined
by one of her entries:

Collecting pebbles for a new mosaic of a world that I could love.

My personal cancer trauma, like Kamienska's—like everyone's—was bounded by trauma in the larger world: the Deepwater Horizon oil spill in the Gulf of Mexico during my diagnosis and treatment, and then, in Hawaii during my recovery, the earthquake and tsunami in Japan.

At my window, in this current bounded moment, a string of twisted, frayed, faded prayer flags sways in a jittery northeast breeze on the day after a 7.8 magnitude earthquake devastated Nepal. Battered prayers for a battered earth.

I pray in words. I pray in poems. I want to learn to pray through breathing, through dreams and sleeplessness, through love and renunciation. I pray through snow that falls outside the window. I pray with the tears that do not end.

That winter in Hawaii, and on into spring, I wrote by day, and in late afternoon, I walked or worked the land or ran. One night, as the sun went down, Craig and I hiked the perimeter of the farm, through the fruit orchard and native tree restoration area to the edge of a gulch and then along a cliff top overlooking the ocean.

At the edge of the gulch, Craig and I stopped to watch the trade-wind-driven waves two hundred feet below collapse against shore. After striking the cliffs, they backwashed, met incoming six-footers, and doubled in size. The coves indenting the cliffs were white and jagged with those pyramids of foam. "Ancient Hawaiians navigated through stuff like that," I said to Craig. Where we stood, Maui was visible across the violence of the Alenuihaha Channel, one of the roughest stretches of water on earth. Dark lines of swells lumbered in parallel to the wind-driven waves, creating even more chaos. The ocean's self-expression: constantly reimagining itself.

I'm moved by everything broken and crippled. Since that's how we really are.

After sushi in town, as we drove back down the hill to the land in the dark, a radio announcer interrupted the symphony playing on Hawaii Public Radio. It took a moment for the words to register. She was issuing a tsunami watch. A massive earthquake had triggered a tidal wave off Japan and if it traveled across the Pacific, it would hit the Hawaiian Islands at 2:00 a.m. When we parked the car and got out, the night was alive with trade winds. The trees were alive and whispering. The clouds were alive, traveling and silent. They streaked past the silent moon, no longer a sliver like two nights ago, now fattened to a slender cantaloupe slice. The ocean two hundred feet below the cliffs was alive, too, a hoary, droning sentience. Our friend Ralph, who lives up the hill, called. The earthquake was an 8.9. The tsunami watch was now a warning. If a wave were to arrive, it would hit Hawaii Island at 3:00 a.m. If a wave were to arrive, it would be the echo of a cry of terrible suffering.

This is no comfort, though, when you howl, yearning for familiar hands, the chest, the one dear body.

"Do you think we should head up the hill?" Craig asked.

"No way," Ralph said. "You're at least two hundred feet above sea level. There ain't gonna be no two-hundred-foot wave."

So we read until we fell into an uneasy sleep, our dreams alive and sent out nightwalking by the trade winds, like everything around us. That belt of ocean covering so much of the earth carried that silent wave, along with its absorbed memory of loss and destruction, across the Pacific through the night while we slept. Above, the cumulous clouds sailed by.

I've always thought of them as sentient, those trade-wind-generated cumulous of the Pacific, parading by so low they seem almost graspable, some nights moon-tinted strangely in shades of olive and burnt orange. I've imagined ancients riding on them, their eyes focused straight ahead, indifferent to what's happening on the islands below, heading forward toward something we can't see. As we slept that night, those clouds, newly populated, sailed by.

My dreams like candles for the dead.

The cell phone rang at 2:00 a.m. It was my sister on Cape Cod. "Are you okay? We were worried. They say a tsunami may hit there in an hour. They mentioned Hawaii and Homer, Alaska, in the *New York Times*." It was 7:00 a.m. on Cape Cod, where she lived then. From their third floor window, each morning for months after my diagnosis, I woke to a view of Cape Cod Bay, a wedge-shaped view of another ocean that caused me only to long for home, the Pacific. I wondered if she stared at that fragment of calm blue bay as she talked to me. After we said good-bye, I stayed awake in the dark for that hour listening to waves churning in the gulch below us. Was it really getting louder, the booming and surging? Was it really subsiding?

On a folding bed, in my heaven, I dreamed my life: I dreamed myself and then the dead man's palm lay on my hair. I was a twelve-year-old widow, who hurried to dream about incomprehensible suffering. Grand-

mother walked 'round all our beds at night, pulling up blankets, touching our foreheads.

At dawn, we woke again and turned on the radio. Waves from Japan had indeed passed by at 3:00 a.m., flooded the lower roads around Kona, flooded a hotel with a foot of seawater, destroyed some beachfront houses. The waves were now heading for the Oregon and Washington coasts. The situation in Japan was much more dire. A twenty-three-foot wave. Hundreds dead, hundreds missing. A nuclear reactor meltdown in progress. All the airports closed. Japanese tourists stranded in Hawaii awaiting news of their loved ones back home.

We cling to words like drowning men to straws. But still we drown, we drown.

Ralph showed up and brought me a book he's been reading called *The Wave.* It's an investigation into monster waves, scientists who study them, ships and crews that go down in them, people who survive them, people who seek them out and ride them on slender boards shaped like slices of fragile moon. Strapped to their lunar slabs, they plunge down seventy-foot wave faces. If you study their faces, captured in surf magazine photos, you see that nothing else exists in their eyes but YES, not even death.

Ralph wanted me to read the chapter about the destruction of Lituya Bay in southeastern Alaska by a locally generated tsunami in the 1950s. An earthquake and ensuing avalanche and the bay's precipitous geology created an eighteen-hundred-foot wave that shaved away forests and stripped bark right off the trees. Well, that's what the geologists said, after studying the aftermath. According to Susan Casey, the author of *The Wave,* the Tlingit people say it's Kah Lituya, Man of Lituya. This sea monster lurks "in the bay's waters, his lair located deep beneath its pinched mouth. Whenever Kah Lituya was disturbed by interlopers or in any way pissed off, he showed his displeasure by rearing up from below, grasping both sides of the bay and shaking them—hard," she writes. I wonder if she's even allowed to tell this story. I wonder if it's bad luck to even read—much less repeat—her words. Two boats anchored in the bay and a man living on Cenotaph, a tear-shaped island in the bay's center, actually survived the wave. Another boat disappeared without a trace.

There is a God of solitude. He covers me closely, like the air. I study Him blindly, by touch. Only His body is everywhere, elusive, impalpable.

In the North Pacific, every so unpredictable often, storms generate freak waves more than a hundred feet high. Every year, despite technology, dozens of ships go down, state-of-the-art container ships, freighters, and tankers slammed by waves like that. Five-hundred-foot-long ships disappear, wiped off the earth with a giant eraser. And we don't even hear about it.

In our bodies, in our lives, every so unpredictable often, storms generate freak waves.

Sometimes I wonder how we survive on this planet. Some of us do for a time, anyway. These forces: storms, tsunamis, cancer, war, earthquakes, volcanoes—they want to tear us apart. Man of Lituya's pissed off brothers, everywhere. From a distance, the planet's so beautiful, it makes big tough astronauts cry. Maybe we survivors hold it in our hearts, the blue-green cloud-swirled earth. It's lodged today under my sternum, a cold sphere of hurt. The clouds keep coming. The one I'm watching has a hole in its center.

The sense of loneliness is an error. We are and move in a great crowd of those who are now, were, and will be.

In that great river.

I arrived in Hawaii feeling fragile, like one of those creatures that's lived out its planktonic, drifting life stage—a barnacle, let's say—and seeks a place to land and transform, turn sessile and strong enough to withstand currents and waves. That winter, I hiked often down into the gulch below our land. One day, I went down there when a high swell was running. It was stormy, the sky gray and angry. I climbed up on a rocky promontory, about fifty feet above the waves. The waves, maybe twelve to fifteen feet tall, lumbered in and crashed below me, sending spray into my face. I inched forward on my hands and knees to peer over, to watch the tops of the waves turn green as they plunged over themselves. Just before they plunged, the crests danced, not in a choreographed way, but in a chaotic desperation, like it was their last moment on earth, which it was, in that waveform. The foam was tinged reddish, as though bloodied, from soil washed off the land. I backed away from the biggest waves, reached my hand behind me to grab the basalt wall. I gasped. The waves cracked. They thundered and pounded, boomed and reverberated. The ground under my feet thrummed. I felt the waves in my throat, in my chest. I found myself laughing crazily, then crying, then terrified, breath entering my body in big, ragged rasps. I felt I'd been led to that place to witness a power bigger than cancer, than death, than courage. *It never stops*, I wrote in my journal later. *It doesn't destroy itself, even with its violence. It dances with its violence. It plunges in on itself, rebounds, roils.* It was a kind of rapture.

So a little spring prays to the ocean, so the beating heart prays to the heart of the universe, so the little word prays to the great Logos, so a dust speck prays to the earth, so the earth prays to the cosmos, so the one prays to the billion, so human love prays to God's love, so always prays to never, so the moment prays to eternity, so the snowflake prays to winter, so the frightened beast prays to the forest silence, so uncertainty prays to beauty itself.

And all these prayers are heard.

Anna Kamienska writes: *For fish death takes the shape of the beautiful white gull with wide-spread wings whose flight we trace with rapture.*

Was she standing beside me, watching those waves? Waves that one day take the shape of a lover, one day a chaos, one day a God, one day a tsunami? Earth, which can break me, which I can hold as a cold marble in my heart. Which are you? Which am I? For a world that I could love, I pray.

The Swan Is How I Know That
I Am Alive

THE SWAN IS A WHITE blur far out in the pond. I don't have my glasses on, so my friend must confirm that it's a swan, not a clot of whipped cream mysteriously dropped from the blue sky onto the pond's surface. It's morning, and we are sitting on a wool blanket drinking tea brewed in a cast iron pot. This is Cape Cod, and this is two years since my breast cancer diagnosis, and this is the second pond of my morning. This is the moment, the present tense. The moment is a swan.

And this is the future, two days later, sitting in the oncologist's office, in my jeans and a hospital johnny, my arms crossed to keep the johnny closed, my sister in a chair against the opposite wall, working on her laptop as we wait for Dr. S—, my oncologist. As always, as he walks through the door, Dr. S— looks for a split second almost startled, then pleased to see us. He is sixty-something, a tad reserved. I want to hug him but can't right now, because if I open my arms, my johnny will open too. And that would be awkward. Because suddenly, the spartan, sterile examination room melts around us, and we're momentarily in another place and situation. Dr. S— sits down and asks me how I am. Not as a doctor, but as though he were just a friend. As though he'd invited us to his house for a visit, and we're sitting in the living room catching up. For a moment, we're just people. Even though he wears a white doctor's coat and there's a stethoscope dangling from his neck and I'm in this cotton garment of the sick—we're just talking about life. All the time we were waiting, anxiety built inside of me. We waited almost an hour to see "the Shnip," as my sister, Mara, affectionately refers to him, shortening his actual name. We always wait a long time here. But rather than let it annoy me, I accept it. Because this is what the Shnip does. He treats you like you're the only patient he has. Or like you've dropped in for a visit at the end of his busy day, and he can finally relax and chat for a while. He told us last time that his wife meditates. I wonder if he's begun practicing meditation. He's that present.

The swan is coming into focus now. I want to write "she," but my friend corrects me. It is probably a male, his mate tucked into some sedge and cattail indentation in the pond's shore, sitting on a clutch of eggs. He patrols the shore always, she says, describing an all-day all-out battle with danger and potential danger he wages with the lake. Like the pair of Canada geese we just watched waddle onto the sand several hundred yards away, the pair he is at this moment beelining toward. He is no decorative swan, spinning slow circles, preening, hoping someone takes his picture. He means business. His focus is impressive. His path is direct. He is intent.

Earlier this morning, after I dropped my sister off at work, I drove to Nickerson State Park. It was unplanned, like this visit with my friend at the swan pond. It was spontaneous. The morning was pure spring: mild, the trees flushed various shades of baby green and speaking in their spring voices, the voices of newly arriving migrant birds. On the radio, I heard that people had been spotting indigo buntings, even one rare black-throated sparrow who normally lives in the desert Southwest. I was going to go to the coffee shop to do some computer work, but I cranked the wheel over at the entrance to Nickerson, thinking I'd walk around Cliff Pond, to breathe the morning air, maybe write in my journal. Cliff Pond had been my refuge during chemo. But something pulled me to another trail, a shorter trail around Little Cliff Pond. In my eight months on the cape, I had never walked that trail. I was the only person in the parking lot between the two ponds. I headed down the trail, pushing through a thicket of birdsong. I found a sandy spot in the woods at the pond's edge, sat down, and pulled out my journal. "Time here now on Cape Cod is stacked many layers deep, the moment dense with past time, with memories of when I lived here during treatment." It's disconcerting. Driving the car down Route 6A was like swimming through a kelp bed. So maybe that's why I walked a new trail, to break out of that viscous sensation of memories sticking around, gummy against the present.

I tell the Shnip it really took a full year, like everyone said, after treatment ended, to feel somewhat "myself" again. "Me and my shadow," I say, the new shadow that now hovers at the edge of my sight, cancer and its uncertainties. He tells me that the shadow will grow paler with time. I believe him, not because he's worked with countless breast cancer patients over the years, but because his wife is a two-time survivor of breast cancer. He knows about the shadow. And I take to the image of a pale shadow. One day, perhaps, it will become a negative of itself, a ghost print, and when I look into it, what will I see? What will it show me?

The swan is not aiming toward those geese after all. He is aiming his prominent orange beak, its black knob, the curve of his forehead, his black eyes, his wings, which my friend observes are never relaxed on his back, always tensed, toward us, the two of us on the blanket, with the pot of tea. I think of a scene in the novel *The Snow Child*, when the girl Faina battles a swan. A swan, as graceful and placid as it appears, is a strong, fierce bird. Its beating wings could break our shins. My friend and I stand. We back away. The swan does not swerve until he's almost grounded himself in the shallows at our feet. Then he turns, eyes us, pushes back off the sand, and begins to forage. We sit back on the blanket. This is the moment, the acute moment of the swan acknowledging us, eye to eye. "I see you, I know you are there, I am aware." It is how I know that I am alive.

An Alaskan friend emailed me this morning of his struggles not to dwell too much in thoughts of mortality. A survivor of one kind of cancer many years ago, recently he's had surgeries to remove melanomas. He's an athlete, a mountaineer. He described to me crashing his bike the other day, blood on his smashed helmet, walking himself and his unscathed bike eight miles back to town. "And I didn't think about it once," he said. Meaning cancer. His body impacting earth, wind moving past his face: it is how he knows he is alive.

The Shnip asks me about Craig, and I tell him it has not been easy on our relationship, cancer and its aftermath, and that only now am I accepting that Craig and I took two separate but parallel journeys out of cancer. Everyone, I say, focuses on the cancer patient and expects partners to be rocks of support. The Shnip says yes, that is the way it is, there are even support groups for partners for that reason. And I tell him we are different, that for Craig, the numbers are his rock of Gibraltar. He is a scientist, I say. And Craig goes back again and again to one scene. When we sat in Dr. S—'s office that first time, two years ago, Mara, Craig, and I listening to his nurse practitioner rattle off my treatment plan. "We don't usually provide numbers unless someone balks at treatment," she said, but she gave them to us nonetheless, the way that each kind of treatment halved the chance of recurrence. And as I sat there, the words and percentages streaming past my ears like twigs in a big, breaking-up northern river, as I sat there ignoring the twigs, fixating instead on the enormous slabs of ice roiling past, Craig looked like a man who'd just lost everything. He leaned forward, his elbows on his knees, face in his big hands. He looked despairing, but he was doing multiplication and addition in his head. Chances of recurrence. Months of treatment. To those prognostic numbers he's returned again and again, lobbing them at my fears. The little sticks bounce off the ice chunks in my head. "For me," I tell the Shnip, "the numbers are no rock."

Now the swan tips up his snow-white tail. He appears to do a headstand, holding the pose for long minutes as he searches the sandy bottom for food. My friend and I talk, drink tea, the swan feeding within a stone's throw. We are suddenly no threat, and I wonder, were we ever? "I think," I tell my friend, "some animals are just more social, some more solitary, than others." I wonder if the swan is lonely. I wonder if he feels more secure in the company of other creatures like us. Why is he feeding right here when there's a whole pond available? I will never know these things. And they are not the point. The swan is the point. The point of this moment. His gleaming black eye. There are no icebergs here, in this moment. There is no fear. No future, no past.

In my journal, at Little Cliff Pond, an hour before the visit with my friend at her pond, an hour before the swan, I wrote, "I want to squeeze as much life out of life as possible. This morning, I am aware, maybe through the birds, and through the distant background hum, a low, human mechanized roar of cars, of the intensity of life, the burning of both candle-ends. I want to squeeze every drop of life out of life, and I want it to squeeze every drop out of me and leave me, at the end, utterly spent, a coat that's lost its animal. I want to be the animal."

"What is your rock?" Dr. S— asks me. Is this the kind of question an oncologist asks? Or a friend?

"Writing is my rock," I say. "The earth is my rock."

"But isn't that painful sometimes?" he asks. "Writing about it? It must be intense, to put those fears down, to go into them, to explore them that way? Isn't it harder?"

"No," I say. "It's harder when I don't. The ungrounded thoughts in my brain are a much worse kind of pain."

The swan is moving gradually away from us now. While he's feeding, his wings relax along his torso, but his black feet move separately to balance the tail tipped up as he feeds deeper and deeper. Now the swan rights himself, and the wings again assume what appears to be a position of tension, of defense. Yet now I see that they also make a basket, a cradle, of the swan's back, in which cygnets could ride, in which something could be carried. The swan swims now for the place where we saw Canada geese earlier. My friend and I talk about the wild, about birdsongs, about the nature of nature, which is not peaceful but incessant, focused, intent on survival, on life. Birds, birds, and the strange birds we are, continuously falling off our bikes so we know that we are alive. Bird hearts beating impossibly fast.

We talk a long time, and then it's time for the Shnip to turn into the doctor again. "Well, let's take a look at you," he says. I sit on the table, and he presses his fingertips into my neck, my sternum. "Breathe," he says, the stethoscope cold on my back. I lie down and he taps his fingers on my abdomen, runs them quickly over the numbness of the scar, presses them up into my armpits. "Okay, you can sit up. You're the picture of health. Go ahead and get dressed." He pulls the curtain to give me privacy. When my sister and I hug him good-bye, he wishes me Godspeed.

Is the incessant rush of nature, the tension, the mad nest building, the desire, life at God speed?

The swan is not a picture of grace or beauty. The swan is flesh and blood, feathers and beak. The swan is now. My friend and I gather up the teapot and cups. We leave the blanket where it is. We say good-bye to the swan and to one another.

At Little Cliff Pond and at my friend's pond, the breeze touched the side of my face and moved on. The birds territorialized—a scratchy, whistley, buzzy, chucking, chattering din—the business and industry and urgency of their brief spans of time on earth. They were not peaceful. Their calls in the forest weren't sweet music to them. The music, as I perceived it, as I loved it, was incidental. They sang work songs, love songs, fight songs. But still, despite all of this urgency of the earth all around, and the urgency inside me, I could finally breathe there, on the pond's edge. I could let the incessant ripples of memory and future flow past my ears, like the ripples on the pond itself, heading across the surface, glancing off this beach, on their way to someplace else. Like the swan, they recognized no edge or ending. They moved forever forward into the next moment.

This is my moment. It is 1:30 a.m. on my forty-ninth birthday. I am in bed listening to the rain. The swan sleeps. We dream each other. I am writing these words: the ice has gone out of the pond. For this moment, the ice has gone out of my life.

49: The Last Five Days

To treat the days like separate lives.
—Seneca

May 5
First bird of the morning:

~ (((((^ ^ ^

I transcribe its song into my notebook. It's been a long winter in the far north, a long time waiting for this sound in the forest. In early May, in coastal Alaska, no matter how keen the wanting, the stingy earth yields so very little. At the end of a day, I make a list of what's been given:

—a few calls of ruby-crowned kinglets
—a few degrees above freezing
—clumps of crocuses spiking through a layer of decayed leaves
—barely perceptible shrinking of snow patches revealing more and more moose-colored ground
—moose-on-moose hue of foraging pregnant moose
—a couple of bewildered yearling moose, shunned and driven off by their mother, scuffing through the alder zone between yard and woods, watching me when I walk to the car

And like these signs, I'm tentatively emerging from my forty-ninth winter on earth.

The silence of these woods unnerves me. Why so few birdsongs? With climate change evident everywhere, it's not a paranoid question. But this anxiety is not environmental. It runs deep: it's my history, my memory. I grew up in the deciduous forest of the northeastern United States, where the trees during the prolonged spring turned green in tiny increments, but the birds arrived en masse. Here in coastal Alaska, it's the reverse: the birches flush green in a matter of days. Now you don't see leaves, now you do. Beginning in April—season of mud and breakup and a blizzard or two—the songbirds trickle in over the course of weeks. I know these things after twenty-four years living here, but still anxious, I listen hard and imagine the bare trees listen back, equally.

Okay, I admit it. There's a lesser reason for my unease. It's five days to my fiftieth birthday. I want to dig my boot heels into the still-frozen earth, delay May 10's arrival. To stretch the moment to its breaking point, to overfill it, that's my drive.

My Latvian immigrant parents each imparted a particular Eastern European pall to birthdays. When I was a child, my father threatened every year to cut our birth dates out of the calendar. The birthdays my mother disliked were her own. For years, we believed she was twenty-nine, until outed by a bank teller asking for her DOB. Forty-seven. We made a fuss right there in the lobby, carrying on all the way to the car, indignant at her deceit, appalled at how old she was. On her sixty-fourth birthday, I called her from Alaska. Afterward, I wrote down her words in my journal, they troubled me so: "I hate my age."

At the time, I thought it tragic. And now, irritating, even enraging. At eighty-six, she still hates her age. To get to be sixty-four! To get to be eighty-six! As a thirty-something, I probably countered her statement with some lame American pop psychology cliché like, "Age doesn't matter, Mom." Or "You are young at heart." What did I know? Another birthday: my sister, in the spirit of enlightening my mother, sent her as a present the book *When I Am An Old Woman, I Shall Wear Purple.* The only purple thing was my mother's anger. She called the lavender-clad feisty crone on the cover an "old bag."

At almost-fifty, can I love my age? Do I understand my forty-nine-year-old heart? If only there were a field guide for the other side of fifty, with handsome illustrations and a handy checklist in the back. Menopause: check. Empty nest: check. Death of first parent: check. Mammogram: check. Breast cancer: check. Chemotherapy, radiation: check. Illusion of immortality lost: check. Spring, and birthdays, and time, and light, and mud, and age—my old field guides are obsolete.

MAY 6

The field guide to birds tells me nothing I don't already know about spring's second migrant, the varied thrush. The bird says:

(tzzzzeeee)   (tzzzzzeee)3

(tzzzzeeee)5

Morning and night, I listen for its electronic buzz. Its familiar call is a relief each spring, especially since my cancer diagnosis. Three years ago, on May 12, I lost my right breast; I lost a beaded string of lymph nodes from my armpit. Each morning, I walk my altered body down the hill to the wetlands, through a dark spruce forest, listening. When I hear it, that rough cry, it's the abrasion of my own physical presence in this world. You're here, bird, another spring. So am I.

If the coastal spruce forest has a voice, this is it, varied thrush calls sketching an acoustic self-portrait of the landscape, pitched variably to reflect dark spaces, thicknesses, the heights of trees. How did I even grasp time and home without these markers? Varied thrushes are nothing like the birds of my youth. These raspy voices don't recall the tender swirlings and whistlings of northeastern species like the red-eyed vireo or the shy veery, high in the budding canopy. No, varied thrush songs describe a plainer face: snowmelt rivulets sluicing through brown meadows, mud to the shins, to the axles, ice jams and overflow, spindly spruce trees swaying in a frigid south wind.

The field guide to birds does provide some pretty body language to describe the varied thrush, a secretive forest bird you rarely see:

nape: bluish gray
eyebrow: a.k.a. supercilium—orange, thin
mask: black around the eye
throat: bright orange
breast band: broad, black

belly: scaled
wings: intricately marked
wingbars: orange

The same bird, over and over, year after year, its song pinning me more tightly to this landscape, thousands of miles away from my birthplace, and I'm more greedy than ever for it. My greed is immense. Varied thrush: current population size twenty-six million, possibly shrinking.

A friend listens to my loss-of-youth fears of turning fifty, tells me to just accept aging (he's in his early forties). No, I won't, I counter, and he raises one dark eyebrow.

MAY 7

This morning, the croaky utterances of sandhill cranes. They nest on the soggy meadows of what's known as the Homer Bench, a rapidly shrinking habitat for birds, a rapidly expanding one for humans. On the bench, humans erect cathedral-like nests, south-facing walls of windows that stare unblinking at Kachemak Bay, Grewingk Glacier, the Chugach Mountains, what realtors call the million-dollar view. How many birds in their exuberance and hurry smack into those windows each spring? Who can say?

No one knows where the sandhills go to roost at night, and I find that comforting. It means the place where I live, populated by an inordinate number of the curious—biologists, writers, artists, birders, retirees—still keeps its secrets. Sometimes I hear the sandhills at dusk (there's no actual night this time of year), flapping over my roof in twilight toward the bluff, and I want to don rubber boots and slog through the drainages after them, find their hidden place. But I know it would be wrong. Because one of the failings of love, and science, and aging, and illness is the breach of the sanctity of secrets, the privacy of the body. Every three months, a sixty-something oncologist passes his fingertips along the bony escarpment where my breast once was, the thin scar, massages the remaining breast, drums at the flesh under my ribs, listening for dull thuds of tumor amid the hollower background acoustics. CT scans expose my insides as gray shades of cirrus and cumulous and dusk-dark. In this age of techno-science, we think everything can be known. But the internal landscape only gets stranger. That was certainly true for my father, whose bizarre utterances in his last years described landscapes and autobiography unknowable to us: a black dog jumping on his bed at night, his bedroom a gas chamber, the imminent arrival of the FBI, his imminent trial for crimes against humanity.

On the other side of fifty, I vow, I'll gather secrets in my coat pockets. But I won't bury them deep in my body, like my father did, and like I have done these forty-nine years. At night I'll release them, so they can roost somewhere where even I can't find them. That's how I saw the tumor in my breast, the swelling, the lump: dark fist of secrets, the body constructing its geode around their hard, dark crystals.

MAY 8

Sometimes it's feathers, not throats, that swell the heart, disturbing the quiet of the subarctic never-night, like the male snipe's love-velocities. I scan the brown field down the muddy road: there . . . and there . . . and there . . . the winnowing produced by his tail feathers as he dives, like the rotoring of a distant, tiny helicopter. For that breathy, whirling sound, he's been called "Heaven's Ram." "Heather-bleater." I never see him, no matter how hard I look. And ravens: water bells and chortlings, but also the heavy whump whump of wings. If a raven flies close overhead, you feel the pressure change inside your ears. Ravens, who stay all year, along with the chickadees and redpolls, fill the winter silence with wingbeats and tentative queries. My queries aren't answered by bird facts; they are only momentarily made irrelevant when I'm stopped in my boot tracks to listen to a sound outside of myself. Rough-and-tumble earth, half thawed, half formed, half broken down, delivers koans for me to ponder on these walks. Like the wall in front of the Zen practitioner, the spaces between trees are where I fix my eyes, count ten breaths, then twenty.

I haven't found the field guide to turning fifty, but surely another one of the chapter titles, besides the one-in-eight chance a woman has of developing cancer in her breast, would be "Losing A Parent." Does the muddy spring earth miss my father's heavy peasant footfalls? Someday, will this icy road miss mine? It's been years since my father's physical body donned an old wool coat and cracked shoes and tramped to the backyard with hedge clippers to bring in the first yellow sprays of forsythia for my mother. Decades since he ordered me out there with a knife to cut a birch switch for my traditional Latvian punishment. Years since he mucked around with a pitchfork in the compost heap, or checked in with his spruce trees and beehives. Since he filled the bird feeders.

Pruned and dusted the orchard. Nature. Birdsong. For his last two years it was more a concept, a wafting, like the first whiff of my mother's black bread baking, not real, just the backdrop for another memory fragment. Because it became winter nonstop for him after a series of mini-strokes precipitated a psychotic break. A kind of brain-blizzard erased all the familiar landmarks. He didn't go outside anymore. He went inside, and was always cold.

One day when I was visiting him in the nursing home on a ninety-degree summer day, his eyes darted to the window.

Is it snowing? Where is your coat?

No, Dad, it's summer.

You must go to the store. And buy me three roses. Red, white, red, for the Latvian flag. Don't forget, red, white, red. Feel my hands, they are already getting colder. Put on your coat. When you come back from the florist, pick up my remains at the front desk.

All those things I thought defined him or gave solace—trees, birds, Catholicism, words—they fled. Like the shrews I evicted a few days ago from the nest they'd made out of chewed up Styrofoam in the bee shed, his preoccupations and passions hightailed it out of him. None of it mattered. None of it sustained. At least not in any visible sense. Only our reassurances eased his constant anxiety. The ten-dollar bill in the desk drawer, yes, Dad, it's there. And Mom, look, there she is across from you in her blue chair. Blink. Blink. Eyes clearing, expression resolving, forward thrust of his body easing back. Familiar faces: wife, daughter. For a few seconds, he was out of the scary, unfamiliar, silent, snowed-in woods in his brain.

I keep coming back to that March three years ago, just weeks before I'd be diagnosed with cancer, when I took that road trip to my old hometown. I parked at the school bus garage, behind the two-acre property that had been my childhood home. I dropped down an embankment into the woods my father had planted. A thousand spruce seedlings crowded onto an acre plot. They were long and spindly, wind soughing through their evergreen tops. Under the canopy, the ground was brown, a thick mat of needles strewn with vodka and beer bottles, the shredded remains of a pup tent. It had become a teenage party hideout. Where the woods ended, I furtively took in the back of the ranch house. It was in need of a paint job. What had been a garden was a weedbed. The orchard was overgrown. I felt nothing of my father's spirit, just its utter absence.

I try to remember birdsong; it must have been there, all around me, but the memory is silent.

MAY 9

As I walk up the road, my breath catches at the ordinary warble of the American robin. The song in this bare forest knits past to present, childhood to middle age, which in my case, with my poor cancer prognosis, is actually old age. In this moment, my edges are defined:

^~'~'~'~'~'~'

No green lawns in Homer in May, no balmy nights. I am wearing ice cleats on my boots, mittens on my hands. The forecast warns of snow. I am listening for birds. I am head-over-heels in love with my life, if not my age, with this dun-colored earth, with the chirs of a flock of tiny redpolls barreling across the field like a tumbleweed. I am trying to come to peace with the way a life vanishes all at once or disappears in tiny increments. I am trying to understand the memory of my father, laid out on a table in the funeral home, in his gray suit, in his maroon woolen vest. His complete absence from that body. My brother slipped a Hershey's chocolate bar and a few dollars in one jacket pocket for his long migration. Into the other pocket I stuffed a plastic baggie of earth, a scoopful of dirt from Kundzeniskis, the now-abandoned farm near Aglona, Latvia, where he was born. When he retired, my father said he wanted to write about Aglona, an ancient peasant town built around a Catholic basilica, purported to be a place of miracles. But the computer discs labeled "My Aglona" that I found among his papers were blank.

Since my cancer diagnosis, I obsess about what traces, if any, we leave behind. There are worse things that could happen than disappearing without a trace, aren't there? Some birds live out their whole lives never having been observed by a human being. Don't they matter? Aren't their lives in fact sacred? Besides, they don't care about our acknowledgment, much less our naming and fact-checking. This is what matters most: the soil of these woods is made, in part, of their skin cells, feathers, and bones.

Perhaps aging gracefully, aging consciously, facing death isn't about acceptance. Keats described negative capability as "the capacity to remain in uncertainties, Mysteries, doubts, without any irritable reaching after fact and reason." Waiting for a spring that won't come, for resolutions that won't reveal themselves, for acceptance, I exist in suspended animation, waiting, one birdcall giving way in its own time to the next, and nothing at rest.

Little life, what do you mean?

^~`~`~`~`~`~`, you say, but I can't help but reach after reason. In two days I'll be fifty, a woman who searches for signs of cancer's return on her body, signs of spring's return on the landscape, balanced like a thrush on a spruce top, checking out the scene below. Everything to my left back there, it's fine, it can stay put, and everything to my right (west? east? which way am I going?) obscured by May snow squalls. I can see myself walking onward with deliberation, considering each forking path (let there still be forks!), naming each bird I hear, leaving behind what I think I understand, until even the calls are unfamiliar. But acceptance? No.

May 10

pthrrrhaaarh phrrraaarh phrraaarh

When I finally went to Latvia, the year before my father died, no bird was familiar. I came to recognize a two-toned corvid, gray and black, the hooded crow. Its rasp sawing through the sandy pine woods along the Baltic Sea coast was the soundtrack for my solitary walks. I came to know the black-and-white stork, who is mute, standing, red leg crooked, atop its ancient stick nest. Its bill-clattering has been likened to the sound of gunfire, a sound my father and mother knew all too well from the war years. My mother was sixteen the day she fled from her home with her family, joining a mass migration of exiles heading south. My father was eighteen when he joined the Waffen SS, the army of Latvia's then occupiers, to fight the wannabe occupiers, the Russians. What he did those years is a secret he muttered out in language scraps throughout my childhood, more so as his dementia deepened. The truth he pocketed and carried with him into the fire when he was cremated. That buried war came back to displace his other loves—the birds, the trees, the earth, the books—to close its walls around him. Watching a father—wounded soldier, cracked librarian, peasant child, alcoholic—warp and dwindle and die: there is no field guide. Even forgiveness seems the feeblest of gestures in the face of such diminishment.

My parents had a secret language, and it was the Latvian folk song. Many *dainas* originated as work songs, born of manual labor in the fields, the boredom and heat and repetition my father knew well. The daily tending of flocks and herds occupied his family. This song, addressed to a rooster, even without translation, resembles birdsong:

> kur tu teci
> kur tu teci,
> gailīti mans?
> kur tu teci,
> kur tu teci,
> gailīti mans?
>
> no rītiņa agrumā,
> no rītiņa agrumā?
>
> ciemā teku,
> ciemā teku,
> meitas celt.
> ciemā teku,
> ciemā teku,
> meitas celt.
>
> no rītiņa agrumā,
> no rītiņa agrumā.
>
> celies mana,
> celies mana līgaviņ,
> celies mana,
> celies mana līgaviņ,
> jau gailītis nodziedāj,
> jau gailītis nodziedāj.

The last part says:

> Wake up my,
> wake up my maiden,
> Wake up my,

> wake up my maiden,
> Already the rooster has sung,
> already the rooster has sung.

My father was mercurial, over-the-top in drunken rage or smoldering depression or rare burst of fine humor. On good days, mornings, he'd burst through our bedroom door, wake us up by crowing in Latvian. *Kikirikee! Kikirikee!* If we failed to rise, humor turned to ire. He held no truck with laziness in his children, with lounging. In my father's world, there was no snooze button. *Ne gulsnaj*, he'd yell from the hall. He called television "the stultifier." He grew up on a peasant homestead, hens and roosters wandering past the front stoop. His father died when he was fourteen. Four years later he was a foot soldier in a brutal war. In a sense, he never woke from that trauma, though he crossed an ocean, learned another language, raised a family on another continent. He never returned to Latvia, even when it gained independence in 1990. Caught between, in a crepuscular life. No *kikirikee* could roust him fully into daylight. No song could carry him back. He used to call my mother an owl when she gazed at him in disapproval. Maybe he was the owl.

I'm building up a lexicon of bird facts, an acoustic repertoire to shore myself against what happened to my father happening to me—exile from the earth. To shore myself against what happened to my mother happening to me—shame at a body aging, dying. I vow I won't forsake nature, won't wear makeup or don a wig, won't shut myself indoors, won't bury my own wars so they haunt me later. I pray nature won't forsake me. For my father, it was human voices not birdsongs that he tuned his ear to in the end: that's the gospel of my father, but I pray it's not for me.

No, wheel me out on my last day to the slough and park me there, for the muck smell and the calls of the white-fronted geese, for the cold east wind on my hands and cheeks. Let there be some wild voice left that I recognize. Even when I've lost all the names.

MAY 11

> craaaaaw craaaaw craaaaw

Hello crow, raucous and ordinary. Hello fifty. Hello now.

TWO

I remembered the bombardment and the great light that preceded it. At first it fell from above, that beautiful, blinding, greenish light, so bright that it seemed to illuminate the earth's every wrinkle. That light illuminates every person, every cell, vein, artery like an x-ray; everything is ready for death. It irradiates and exposes all that is hidden most deeply—terror, the body's animal terror.

—Anna Kamienska

When What I Feared Most Came to Pass

WHEREVER THERE IS SPRING ON earth, it's associated with rebirth, with youth, with new life. When what I feared most came to pass, it was spring. Cancer was reborn in me as life was reborn in the earth. More likely, reborn is not the word, but reawakened. It had been dormant, like a crocus bulb, like a fern rootstock, for two and a half years. Life poses unanswerable question after question, and one of mine is, why in spring? What could it mean? The first time, and second, why did my death step forward in spring like the young moose that haunted our neighborhood that April, newly rejected by its mother, who was pregnant with the nervous yearling's sibling?

It was a cool May in 2013 in Homer, Alaska, everything late—the leaves, the flowers—rain alternating with snow or hail alternating with sun, sometimes all within a single hour. I took to writing in our greenhouse while weather happened outside. I wrote in the company of the flower starts I'd replanted in the hanging baskets and window boxes that would decorate our deck once it warmed up. No leaves yet on the birches surrounding our house, just a little unfurling green on the elderberry and gooseberry bushes, and on the moose-chewed May trees. In that humid, light-filled, earth-smelling shelter, it was warm and enclosed, but I could still hear birdsong. It was all around, the birds really going at it despite the weather, building nests, chasing off intruders into their territories. So much to do in the short subarctic summer, and they were doing it. The greenhouse was one of the places I felt most at peace in my growing physical unease, along with the quiet beach I walked to town sometimes, or the forest and swamp boardwalk trail down the road. The greenhouse reflected the Latvian peasant in me, the simple old summer dachas of my friends in Latvia, my father's style of patched-together workmanship. My window boxes were made of unvarnished graying scrap lumber. The table holding the long boxes of nasturtiums was built out of swaybacked plywood supported by six defunct tires.

I started keeping a book in the greenhouse that spring, and I'd sit in a folding chair after planting seeds or weeding the window boxes and read at random from it and then pick up my computer and write. By now, that book is swollen with moisture, a few of its pages stuck together. The book contains writings and thoughts and poems of Stanley Kunitz, a poet who was a meticulous New England gardener. It's called *The Wild Braid: A Poet Reflects on a Century in the Garden*. Kunitz died at age 101. At 100, when he wrote the book with the help of a friend, he was still gardening (and still writing poems). Having come out of a nearly fatal illness, he told a friend, "Ahh, I feel I've gone through a whole transformation . . . it's a sense of being in control of your world, and going where you want to go. . . . A feeling of power instead of feeling a victim." The photos in the book show opulent gardens of his Provincetown, Massachusetts, home— Victorian spillover gardens of anemone, foxglove, bearded iris—things we only dream of up here in the north, at least until climate change alters our winters sufficiently. And yet I did dream of them that spring, dreamed of a poet's flower gardens, and my mother's flower gardens, her primroses and tulips, her roses and lilies of the valley, her wild trillium transplanted from the woods near my childhood house, her rock garden plants, her mums. See, while my father was a child of peasant farmers in rural Latvia, my mother was the child of upper-middle-class town dwellers, and I am made of both of them. The funky greenhouse is my father in me, while my desire for lush flowerbeds is my mother in me. My plan that spring was to consolidate into just a couple of beds my widely spread out perennials, which bloomed in one mainly purple exuberance in spring then toppled into disarray, overtaken by chickweed and nettles by midsummer. Maybe I could actually nurse them along into something like order. Perhaps if I contented myself with less, I thought, something opulent and lush would grow up in that more intimate space, would bloom on into fall.

At the same time I sought the comfort of the rustic, non-opulent, funky greenhouse with its piles of pots, its rough-cut lumber beds of soil Craig dug from under the elderberries. He'd hauled the dirt from the thicket in salvaged five-gallon pails repurposed for tomatoes, and I'd mixed that dirt with composted fish from a farm up the road and compost from our own heap and fish fertilizer. Ragged old pieces of shade cloth kept the young plants warm at night, as the temperature still dipped down into the thirties. I'd been calling it a recalcitrant spring, and in town you heard a lot of moaning. When I considered the temperature in the landscape of my youth, western New York, where my mother had gardened, I truly felt like I was orbiting some other, shyer sun.

In the greenhouse, there was earth but also words. In the greenhouse I was not only having a conversation with my own blank pages, but with everything going on outside me, even with the planes that took off from the Homer airport and headed to Anchorage, and also with *The Wild Braid*. At one hundred, Stanley Kunitz wrote, "The storm we had the other day was rather spectacular; I felt it was somehow a message. It seemed so threatening at first, and then suddenly it was just a little downpour. And then it dissolved into a quite peaceful late afternoon. I interpret it positively. I had felt a sense of foreboding, certainly for the last few months, and psychologically this seemed to say, 'Stop thinking negatively about whatever's happening now. Find out what you can do, and do it.'"

It had been for me a rough patch physically: I'd felt oddly in my body, much as I had during chemotherapy three years before. I could only eat certain foods, felt uncomfortable in my body much of the time, breathed hard after climbing a set of stairs. My usual physical routines had been interrupted. I'd stopped running, then stopped climbing hills on walks. I'd been misdiagnosed with various afflictions, as the doctors ruled out the simplest explanations, the not-cancer options falling and falling away, one by one.

All the while, that young moose snorted in the elderberry thickets, bolted with hackles raised at my car driving up our road. When I'd roll down the window to speak reassuringly, it glared at me, flour-scoop ears laid back, eyes white rimmed. I kept my gaze focused on the up close. I held myself steady, focused on what my body could still do. I walked a two-mile swamp trail, pausing at every bench to catch my breath. I watered plants in the greenhouse. On sunny days, planting seeds in the garden, I lay down to rest on the black dirt of the paths between beds. Something in me said *be totally present*, so I tried.

In my journal, I struggled to find the meaning in feeling so lousy for months. Since cancer treatment, writing had been so much about finding meaning, on telling a coherent rebirth story. But something shifted in the greenhouse when one afternoon I read a paragraph of *The Wild Braid*: "There's a conversation that keeps going on beyond the human level, in many ways, beyond language, extending into the atmosphere itself. Weather is a form of communication. There is an exchange between the self and the atmosphere that sets the tone for an entire day. The changeability, its overwhelming range of possibilities, exercises a more defined influence on human moods than perhaps anything." In the greenhouse, that conversation was plain to me. It was bigger than the ongoing conversation I held with my body, with my fear. The conversation manifested as the rhythm of the rain, which waxed and waned; as bird-spats among the robins, the fox sparrows, the varied thrushes; as humidity and as the smell of damp, rich soil. No matter what was happening in my body, I could be part of that conversation, and that conversation included birth and death and desire. Especially desire. "'Desire,'" wrote Kunitz, "is one of the strongest words in the language, which is why . . . as I look back on it, the very sound of that word is a cry." I heard that cry, though I couldn't decipher what my body was telling me or translate it into language. But the earth knew. The young, agitated moose knew. The rain knew, the birds knew, and so, when I look back on it, I knew too. It was what I had feared most, and it was happening, but the way I had imagined it was nothing like how it was happening, so I didn't recognize it. I was planting seeds. I was writing in the greenhouse. I was reading the words of a very old man and relating to what he was saying. All of the things I'd accumulated in my life—the furniture, the sentimental rocks, my mother's teacups, the rows and rows of books, the knowledge, the clothes, the telephone—felt a world away, even though they filled our home, just up the driveway from the greenhouse. All I needed was a cheap canvas chair, the songs of birds, a shelter from the rain, the life of plants I'd tended from seeds, the dirt under my fingernails, one book open in my lap, and connection with the humans and creatures I loved.

And when the actual day came, the day I knew with my brain what the earth had been telling me, that what I feared most had come to pass, it came first as words. Though I'd long imagined and feared receiving those words—words like *recurrence*—when they came, it was nothing like I'd imagined. That is, after the delivery of the news, which came for the most part as expected, as foreign language, the lexicon of disease and medicine followed by the familiar language of sorrow. The news came by way of the telephone, the specific language of one particular disease delivered by my doctor, news of the specific breast cancer inside me, my cancer. *Adenocarcinoma of the breast. Malignant pleural effusion. Metastasis. I am sorry.* I'd lived long enough to know that what our minds invent out of the tendrils of our fears, those mental inventions bear little resemblance to what's real. I had imagined falling to my knees. I had imagined myself curled up in terror. I had imagined my heart galloping out of my mouth. I had imagined a sensation of falling, even of failure. I had imagined hope flushing out of my body and running off like too-early rain on still-frozen earth, leaving behind a dangerous ice sheen that can be mistaken for wetness.

After I hung up the phone, I sat for a moment at the kitchen table, staring out at the bare birch trees. I gave myself over to the rush of breath like rain that carried me past the doctor's words and into the next moment, and that moment was the earth, where rain goes when it finds its way past an obstruction. It goes in. It finds that way. I felt a strange relief.

Then, I gathered my words. "Craig," I called to my husband, "Craig, come here."

"What's going on?" he said, walking downstairs, walking to where I sat at the kitchen table, my head now resting on my arms.

"It's the cancer," I said. "The cancer's back." And I broke down then. And he sat heavily down beside me as the words closed in.

When what I feared most came to pass, for a while that day, it seemed that Craig and I had been ushered onto a tiny boat, maybe the size of a rice cake, and pushed off shore by an indifferent stranger. A current soon carried us far into a fog. We clung to each other. We stared for hours into the fog, not seeking anything solid, not trying to see. We drifted. Jags of crying came on like squalls, passed, leaving us empty, dripping. When what I feared most came to pass, I felt oddly calm. Everything slowed down.

When what I feared most came to pass, for hours, Craig and I sat in the living room, staring out the window. At one point I thought (and tried to say) what I never imagined I'd say after receiving such news: *I've been given a heaven on earth. I've lived in paradise. I've had everything. There's nothing I want, nothing I'd change, nowhere I'd go.* My desire was for more of what I'd been given, more forest garden stream melt poplar-bud crane thrush mud puddle nettle moss waterfall. It overran itself, my desire. My desire brimmed like water up against an ice dam. My desire felt dangerous.

When what I feared most came to pass, Craig and I dragged an old quilt and the comforter and pillows from our bed into the backyard. It was a warm afternoon by then. We lay the quilt on the ground near the garden and covered ourselves with the comforter and held each other and listened to the birds nattering on in the leafless forest canopy, listened to what would continue on with or without us. In the evening, I knelt in the garden and planted tarragon. I looked at the spindly starts and thought, *creation.* I thought, *faith.* So blind, so foolish. I went to the greenhouse. I watered the tomatoes. I stared at the baby green of their hairy leaves. "This is all we have, right now, right here," I said to Craig. I knew everything I'd read of Buddhism to be absolutely true. There is no future. There was only the salad Craig made for me. There were my lungs, freed of the malignant fluid that had been gradually choking me, drained by doctors a few days before, three liters of fluid the color of swamp water that had filled three glass bottles. There were my lungs, now filling completely with breath. I experienced a grace-of-only-the-moment in the moment and then the moment passed into another. And what I feared most came and kept coming, and its form kept changing.

When what I feared most came to pass, I emailed my oncologist in Boston, where I'd been treated two years prior, with the news of my pathology results. Dr. S— called me, told me it was a time for courage and hope. Oncologists are peddlers of hope, someone said, cynically. Yet I trusted Dr. S—, who'd worked in the field for decades, whose own wife was a two-time breast cancer survivor. I bought what he peddled. And because I trusted it equally, I listened to the earth, to the voice of spring, and it spoke of a hopeless hope. The lives of birds are short and furious. They seemed to be singing of my impending losses, all the things that are mine only for the moment. I took a hike with my stepdaughters, one of them five months pregnant, and we headed up a trail through wet brown meadows, and wherever I spotted a bracket fungus clamped to a tree within reach, I scratched the word "hope" or the word "faith" into its underside with my fingernail. I hoped for the moment I was living, that was all; that was enough.

On the cover of *The Wild Braid*, Stanley Kunitz wears a blue-and-black plaid flannel shirt and tan corduroy pants. He leans over to inspect some ferns and petunias, yet one can see that his back, even when he's not leaning over, is bent forward. Like a peony heavy in its late flowering, gravity draws his head and heart toward the earth.

When breast cancer comes back in this way, it is incurable; it is terminal. What is healing, what is spring, in that context? What is hope? Spring is not an endpoint; neither is fall. They are part of a round. No two springs the same; different birds arrive to nest, different moose stalk the edges. Nature is contingency, not progress. Change is the only unchanging variable. Healing is a labyrinth, not a restoration project.

As I lived forward from the day when what I feared most came to pass, people would sometimes call me brave. A woman would say, "I'm so impressed with how you keep doing things, living life," and I felt my hackles rise. What alternative did I have? Start to dig my own grave in the deep soil of the woods behind my house? It seemed at times a linear question I had to answer, for how to move forward—plan to live, or plan to die? It took two years of living with metastatic cancer to recognize there was no difference, to recognize that living is not separate from dying. It is not yet time to dig a grave, but time to wander the woods, seeking a good site. It is time to gather all I love most around me. It is time, as always throughout my life, to write. A time to remake the flower beds into something I can tend. A time to redefine the word *hope*.

"We have storms and stresses and positive indications and negative indications that affect us every day. Each of us is a very sensitive keyboard," wrote the hundred-year-old gardener, the poet, stooped there among his flowers, standing at the ecotone between being here and not being here. So sensitive that a molecule of compost scent could spark a poem. He wasn't without fear. And when what he (we) feared most came to pass, in the absolute, mortal instant, I pray it was beyond anything he imagined.

Wild Darkness

FOR TWENTY-SIX SEPTEMBERS I'VE HIKED up streams littered with corpses of dying humpbacked salmon. It is nothing new, nothing surprising, not the stench, not the gore, not the thrashing of black humpies plowing past their dead brethren to spawn and die. It is familiar; still it is terrible and wild. Winged and furred predators gather at the stream mouths to pounce, pluck, tear, rip, and plunder the living, dying hordes. This September, it is just as terrible and wild as ever, and also new. I gather in the scene with different eyes, the eyes of someone whose own demise is no longer an abstraction, the eyes of someone who's experienced the tears, rips, and plunder of cancer treatment. In spring, I learned my breast cancer had come back, had metastasized to the pleura of my right lung. Metastatic breast cancer is incurable. Through its prism I now see this world.

I'm not a salmon biologist. I don't hike salmon streams as part of my job. I hike up streams and bear trails and muskegs and mountains for pleasure. The work my husband and I do each field season in Prince William Sound is sedentary. We study whales. For weeks at a stretch, we live on a thirty-four-foot boat far from any town, often out of cell phone and Internet range. We sit for hours on the flying bridge with binoculars or a camera pressed to our eyes. Periodically, we climb down the ladder and walk a few paces to the cabin to retrieve the orca or humpback catalog, to drop the hydrophone, or to grab fresh batteries, mugs of hot soup or tea, or granola bars. We climb back up. We get wet, we get cold, we get bored; sometimes we even get sunburned. But we don't get exercise. We eat, sleep, and work on the boat. Hikes are a part of our daily round, our sanity, our maintenance. We hike because we love this rainy, lush, turbulent, breathing, expiring, windy place as much as we love our work with whales. It's a good thing, because weather thwarts our research half the time in autumn and sends us ashore, swaddled in heavy raingear, paddling against williwaw gusts and sideways rain in our red plastic kayaks. What we find there is not always pretty.

Normally, September is the beginning of the end of our field season, which starts most years in April or May. But for me this year, it's the beginning, and conversely, like everything else in my life since I learned cancer had come back, it's tinged with the prescience of ending. The median survival for a person with metastatic breast cancer is twenty-six months. Some people live much longer. An oncologist told me he could give me a prognosis if I demanded one, but it would most likely be wrong. I changed the subject. No one can tell me how long I will live. Will this be my last field season? Will the chemo pill I'm taking subdue the cancer into a long-term remission? Will I be well enough to work on the boat next summer? Will I be alive?

A summer of tests and procedures and doctor appointments kept me off the boat until now. A surgery and six-day hospitalization in early August to prevent fluid from building up in my pleural space taught me that certain experiences cut us off entirely from nature—or seem to; I know that as long as we inhabit bodies of flesh, blood, and bone, we are wholly inside nature. But our brains, under medical duress, forget this. Flesh, blood, and bone notwithstanding, a body hooked by way of tubes to suction devices, by way of an IV needle to a synthetic morphine pump forgets its organic animal self. In the hospital, I learned to fear something more than death: existence dependent upon technology, machines, sterile procedures, hoses, pumps, chemicals easing one kind of pain only to feed a psychic other. Existence apart from dirt, mud, muck, wind gust, crow caw, fishy orca breath, bog musk, deer track, rain squall, bear scat. The whole ordeal was a necessary palliation, a stint of suffering to grant me long-term physical freedom. And yet it smacked of the way people too often spend their last days alive, and it really scared me.

Ultimately, what I faced those hospital nights, what I face every day, is death impending—the other side, the passing over into, the big unknown—what poet Joseph Brodsky called his "wild darkness," what poet Christian Wiman calls his "bright abyss." Death may be the wildest thing of all, the least tamed or known phenomenon our consciousness has to reckon with. I don't yet—might not ever—understand how to meet it. I stumble toward it in dusky conifer light. Or perhaps (I tell myself), though we deny and abhor and battle death in our society, though we hide it away, it is something so natural, so innate, that when the time comes, our bodies—our whole selves—know exactly how it's done. All I know right now is that something has stepped toward me, some invisible presence in the woods, one I've always sensed and feared and backed away from, calling out in a tentative voice, "Hello?" I've tried to scare it off, but I now must approach my own predatory, furred, toothed, clawed angel. Despite my advanced degrees in biology and creative writing, despite more than two decades observing orcas and humpback whales in the field, for such an encounter, my mind and eyes are utterly unschooled.

No one teaches us how to die. No one teaches us how to be born, either. In an essay about visiting the open air cremation pyres of Varanasi, India, Pico Iyer quotes the scholar Diana L. Eck: "For Hindus, death is not the opposite of life; it is, rather, the opposite of birth." It happens that my stepdaughter Eve is pregnant. I've known her since she was three years old; she's thirty now. One late afternoon this spring, early in her pregnancy, early in my diagnosis, we picked bags of wild rose petals together in a meadow below my house. She intended to make rose-flavored mead. We hadn't talked much about the implications of my cancer recurrence; in the meadow, we almost didn't have to. It hovered in the honeyed sunlight between us. That light held the fact of life growing inside her and cancer growing inside me equally, strangely. We talked around the inexplicable until, our bags full of pale pink petals, we held each other in the tall grass and cried. Watching her body change in the months since, without aid of technology or study or experience, watching her simply embody pregnancy, should teach me something about dying. In preparation for giving birth, she reads how-to books, takes prenatal yoga, attends birthing classes. She studies and imagines. Yet no matter how learned she becomes, how well informed, with the first contraction, her body will take over. It will enact the ancient, inborn process common to bears, goats, humans, whales, and field mice. She will inhabit her animal self. She will emit animal cries. She will experience the birth of her child; she will live it. Her body, not her will or her mind or even her self, will give birth to a baby.

Can I take comfort in the countless births and deaths this earth enacts each moment, the jellyfish, the barnacles, the orcas, the salmon, the fungi, the trees, much less the humans? I woke this morning listening to the screech of gulls from the stream mouth. We'd anchored in Sleepy Bay for the night, a cove wide open to the strait where we often find orcas. The humpbacked salmon—millions returned this summer, a record run—are all up the creeks now. Before starting our daily search, Craig and I kayaked to shore. As we approached, I watched the gulls, dozens of them, launching from the sloping beach where the stream branched into rivulets and poured into the bay. They wheeled and dipped over our heads; quickly they settled again to their grim task, plucking at faded carcasses of dead salmon scattered all over the stones. The stench of a salmon stream in September is a cloying muck of rot, waste, ammonia. Rocks are smeared with black bear shit, white gull shit. This is in-your-face death, death without palliation or mercy or intervention. This mass death of salmon is at the same time enlivening, feeding energy to gulls, bears, river otters, eagles, and the invisible decomposers who break the carcasses down to just bones and scales, which winter erases. This same stream in spring is clear cold water I kneel and drink from or plunge my head into. It is snowmelt and rain filtered through alpine tundra, avalanche chute, muskeg, fen, and bog, water fresh, alive, and oxygenated, water newborn, rushing over clean stones, numbing my skin.

After we dragged the kayaks above tideline, Craig left me alone at the stream mouth and wandered down the beach to retrieve a five-gallon bucket he'd spotted. Normally, I am nervous about bears. But this time I walked up the stream toward the woods without singing or calling out. I stood on the bank and watched the birth-death spectacle. When Craig joined me I uttered this platitude: "We have separated ourselves so much from nature." I didn't say what I really meant. I rarely do these days. I fear that most people, even those who love me best, would think me morbid if they could read my thoughts. Sometimes, with Craig, I imagine he hears the words beneath my words, knows my mind, and then, silence seems the form of conversation. What I really meant was that despite the lack of palliation or mercy or intervention, I envied those salmon their raw deaths, not for a moment separated from nature, not even when dragged from their element by a bear. I thought about my childhood cat Mince, who, when she got sick, wandered off into nature to die. She didn't want our comfort. She reverted to her primal nature. My mother told me that was what animals did. They died in private. I imagined Mince's brindled form camouflaged in a bed of leaf litter deep in the neighbor's blackberry bramble thicket. I confess. I have imagined myself laid out naked on a muskeg, shuddering in my last moss-and-tannin-infused breath.

I know, I know. Dying of cancer in a bog would not look or sound pretty or peaceful. Hidden from view in this dream scene is the suffering, is the agony. Is the needle, and the morphine pump, unavailable to the salmon, eyeless, its wordless mouth opening and closing, body swaying in its tattered whitening skin.

I don't by any means think constantly about dying. My reality is dual: one foot firmly in the living stream, the other on the gory bank. Life has become vivid and immediate these last months. No years of Buddhist meditation got me to this place, just words on the phone: the cells were malignant. Later that day, after the crying, after sitting mutely on the living room couch and staring out the window, Craig and I hauled a quilt into the backyard and lay down on the ground at the edge of the woods. We curled up, listening to wind in the birch leaves, the frenetic din of territorial birds staking their claims. Spring sprung on while we dozed off. Staying in the present moment isn't difficult when the alternative is dire: useless imaginings of what might or might not come to pass. When I woke this morning, my mind darted down the dying-of-cancer path, as it does every morning, and I reeled it back by reminding myself of a poem by the late Jane Kenyon, called "Otherwise."

> I got out of bed
> on two strong legs.
> It might have been
> otherwise.

Kenyon died of cancer when she was about my age. She ends the poem: "But one day, I know / it will be otherwise." Her words in the back of my mind, I talked myself home to the real. Right now, Eva, you are here, listening to gulls shrieking on the beach. Right now, your two legs, your two arms, your two lungs, your beating heart will carry you under your own power up the salmon stream into the woods where the blueberries are ripe. You will pick gallons to freeze, a bulwark shored against winter's want, against a dearth of hope.

Craig and I hiked up the creek a ways to where a path led into the forest, where blueberry bushes grew along the margins of bog. It wasn't a pleasant way to get there. The rocks were slick with decay, the water rushing and tea colored from weeks of rain. The stink was thick as syrup around us, unrelenting. I stepped around half-consumed corpses, bent and sloughing skin, over eyeless heads, headless flanks, brainless skulls, pearly backbones stripped of meat. As we crossed the creek, live humpies thumped my ankles, then battered the rocks to get away. In their singular drive to spawn, they plowed right through eddies of bleached-out dead, as if that fate were not meant for them. Pico Iyer describes the charnel grounds along the banks of the Ganges in this way: "Spirituality in Varanasi lies precisely in the poverty and sickness and death that it weaves into its unending tapestry: a place of holiness, it says, is not apart from the world, in a Shangri-la of calm, but a place where purity and filth, anarchy and ritual, unquenchable vitality and the constant imminence of death all flow together." If there is spirituality in nature, it is in the sublime purity of wild roses and wild mushrooms in mossy woods and the vitality of deer nibbling kelp on the beach and the violet light of an oncoming storm, and equally in the anarchy and filth of the spawning grounds, in the undoctored real of the ever-dying world.

Several days ago, I read an essay by Robert Hass, in an anthology of ecopoetry. He mentioned Bill McKibben's seminal 1989 book *The End of Nature*, in which McKibben confronts a new reality, a world in which human impact alters even the once-untamed force of weather. Our dominion over the earth, our global reach, our altering of climate, our acidification of the rain and the ocean, our mass poisoning of the communal food supply, means nature as we once conceived it—bigger than us, out of our control, pure and free—is over. Nothing on this earth is apart from human tinkering. No raindrop falling on my face is free of human causation. Even my body, burdened with cancer, burdened with fifty years' worth of toxins, enacts this truth. My greatest fear is a variation of McKibben's revelation: that the end of nature means the end of natural death, natural return to earthly elements. I read his book years ago. My new eyes see it differently, and maybe you can't trust the perceptions of someone like me, desperately seeking meaning in the face of metastatic cancer, in the face of personal extinction. But I will give you my scouting report just the same. Watching those salmon, stepping around their wrecked, spent flesh, I kept thinking, "No one told them. No one told these fish, or their predators—the bears, the gulls, the eagles, the microbes—that nature is over. They don't get it." No one told the cancer in my body either. Oncologist and writer Siddhartha Mukherjee calls cancer "the emperor of all maladies," for its ability to confound everything the human mind can hurl at it.

In "King of the River," a poem by Stanley Kunitz, he too watches salmon battling up a stream, and the parallel he draws with human life and striving and passion and aging is tight and explicit and maybe even a little overwrought. At least I saw it that way when I first read the poem. I was in my thirties then, and my health was a given. Now the poem reads more like a Biblical truth. "The great clock of your life / is slowing down, / while the small clocks run wild." These great clocks and small clocks are the very texture of our days on earth. Yet for most of us, most of the time, they tick on unheard. In the society in which I live, in that other world, across the mountains—far from this wild place where death is explicit and occurs in plain sight, where it is ordinary and everyday and unremarkable—people don't talk about dying. People rarely witness the dying of their fellow humans (much less the animals they eat). Special people minister to the dying. Sometimes people in their travail fly overseas and pay strangers to hasten their dying. We have no charnel grounds, only cemeteries, shaded by big trees, mowed and tended by groundskeepers. Or we're handed the ashes of our loved ones in sealed urns or handsome boxes, to disperse at sea or from mountain peaks.

Facing death in a death-phobic culture is lonely. But in wild places like Prince William Sound, and the woods and sloughs behind my house, it is different. The salmon dying in their stream tell me I am not alone. The evidence is everywhere: in the skull of an immature eagle I found in the woods, in the bones of a moose in the gully below my house, in the corpse of a wasp on the windowsill, in the fall of a birch leaf from its branch. These things tell me death is true, right, graceful, not tragic, not failure, not defeat. "For this you were born," writes Stanley Kunitz. For this you were born, say the salmon. A tough, gritty fisherman friend I knew in my twenties called Prince William Sound "God's country." It still is, and I am in good company here.

We have no dominion over what the world will do to us, all of us. What the earth will make of our tinkering and abuse can be modeled by computers but in the end is beyond our reckoning, our science. Nature is not simply done to. Nature responds. Nature talks back. Nature is willful. We have no dominion over the wild darkness that surrounds us. It is everywhere, under our feet, in the air we breathe, but we know nothing of it. We know more about the universe and the mind of an octopus than we do about death's true nature. We know only that it is terrible and inescapable, and it is wild.

Death is nature. Nature is far from over. In the end, the gore at the creek comforts more than it appalls. In the end—I must believe it—just like a salmon, I will know how to die, and though I die, though I lose my life, nature wins. Nature endures. It is strange, and it is hard, but it is comfort, and I'll take it.

The Truth About Jesus

THE CALL COMES FIVE MINUTES before yoga, just as I'm pulling into
the parking lot. It's my friend Ralph from Hawaii, who's just finished
a ten-day meditation retreat, and his voice is shaky. I know that skin-
less feeling, reentering the world after time in wilderness or meditation
or some other kind of isolation, some "narrow road to the interior," as
seventeenth-century Japanese poet Basho called his solo pilgrimage on
foot, undertaken right before he died. "I'm back to living alone on the
land," Ralph says, his words catching as his tears come on. His eighteen-
year-long relationship ended this past winter. I read a story recently of
one woman's recovery from an abortion trauma, the healing ritual her
friends enacted for her after the ordeal, and what they said at its close:
"The ritual begins *now*."

A sadness maybe in its sense of isolation here where nature's darker spirits
hide—like a strange and beautiful woman whose heart has been broken.
                                                                —Basho

It was misty the morning I left Bainbridge after two weeks of cancer
appointments in Seattle, waiting for results at my sister's house on the

island. I left Mara standing on the ferry ramp, and I stood on the bow, watching until fog blotted her out. We'd been through more than the usual load of cancer trouble together this go-around: holding her hand through a procedure to draw four liters of malignant fluid out of my abdomen; waiting for pathology results on the fluid; waiting for my oncologist to decide how to control my ever-evolving metastatic breast cancer; wondering why I felt zinging, diffuse, nervy pains in my pelvis. And then, untethered, heading back to Alaska for three months to resume some version of my life. *The ritual begins now.*

In wilderness, the earth supports solitude. In yoga, the sangha, the community of practitioners, supports practice. And then you walk out the door.

> *It's good now and then*
> *to go out snow-viewing*
> *until I tumble.*
> —Basho

On the train to the SeaTac Airport, I wondered what to make of a billboard for one of the city's research centers: *We can see the end of cancer from here.* I took in the grungy station as we pulled away. From where I sat, with my terminal diagnosis, the only end I could see was the end of *my* cancer, which was coupled completely with the end of me. So much knowledge amassed. Yet no way for science to fix a bollixed up tumor-suppressor gene like mine. For so many with cancer, decades-old chemo drugs that indiscriminately kill fast-growing cells (not only cancer, but hair, mucus membrane, skin, nerves), drugs derived from things like mustard gas, are still the standard of care. I flashed back to the little bald girl Mara and I saw in a wheelchair outside the cancer center; her oxygen tubing taped to her face with colorful Band-Aids; her cheerful leopard print tights clinging to her skinny legs. It seems we want cheery, brave cancer patients—at least that's how they appear "in the literature," in the chemo pamphlets and on the billboards. Just look at the products in the cancer stores on oncology floors: witty cancer-themed nightgowns, jaunty coffee cup slogans like "I didn't survive cancer to die of stress!"; makeup sessions to improve our self-esteem; bright scarves and flower-appliquéd hats to conceal our bald heads. Once, a friend sent me a *Yoga Journal* article about a teacher photographed in various yoga poses on an infusion room recliner, bald and buff and glowing, an IV tube slinking up her arm to its chemo bag. She was being treated for early stage breast cancer. If I hadn't gone through it myself, strong going into chemo from my own years of yoga and long-distance running and an organic food diet, I might have found the image empowering. Instead I wondered where in the images were hints of the nausea, fatigue, neuropathy, reflux, mouth sores, skin rashes, anemia-pale skin I had known and witnessed in my fellow patients.

Wait. I don't want to tell a bummer victim cancer story. But there were so many people yesterday at the cancer center who looked resigned, not perky, leaning on walkers, dozing in wheelchairs, swaying at reception counters, waiting for another infusion or procedure or blood draw. There was the little girl slouched in her wheelchair, so thin, so pale.

I can't write a heroic, peppy cancer story, though. I'm sorry, I can't. The ritual should begin now, but I can't think of a ritual to make any of this okay.

I tell Ralph I have to go: yoga is about to start. "There's one more thing I have to tell you," he says. "I have some sad news. Kea died."

Though I balk, though I say, "What?" and "No!" though my throat seizes up, I'm not completely surprised. Kea, a border collie mongrel, arrived tentatively on the thirteen-acre farm my husband and I share in winter with Ralph. She arrived abandoned by her people, who'd fled the lava flow threatening their home. She arrived timid, hiding much of the day under Ralph's house. She arrived as though fully aware of contingency. I befriended Kea, drew her out, took her on hikes, and eventually she moved over to our house. Ralph, a wiry, sixty-seven-year-old farmer and sailor and builder with a six-pack and more stamina than most twenty-somethings, didn't take to Kea. She wouldn't work. Wouldn't chase the geese who liked to congregate and poop on his lanai, wouldn't herd sheep escaped from the pasture, wouldn't bark at arriving cars or feral pigs wandering in the night. She wanted only to connect to a human. That human became me. Through that winter's every-three-week cycling through chemo side effects, she accompanied me everywhere I went—my trudges around the yard on bad days, my eight-mile treks on good. She seemed much older than her three years. She had melancholy eyes. She hung her head low like a coyote when she trotted beside me, in a sly-shy way checking on my progress every few minutes with her skulky backward glances.

Within this temporal body composed of a hundred bones and nine holes there resides a spirit which, for lack of an adequate name, I think of as windblown. Like delicate drapery, it may be torn away and blown off by the least breeze.

—Basho

How do I spin this story to give it some uplift? How do I tell a metastatic cancer story that's true, useful, inspiring, when I can't offer news of success, of victory? My tumor markers have spiked. An ultrasound revealed some fluid re-accumulating in my pelvis. As Christopher Hitchens said in his book *Mortality*, "I'm not fighting a battle with cancer; it's fighting a battle with me." But that's not right either. Cancer is indifferent, not malicious. It is not mean or evil, no more so than a tsunami or hurricane. It's a force of nature unleashed from some unknown point of origin. Genetically, it's bad luck, a recent study reported. Some cancers are preprogrammed to spread. Battle or no battle, Hitchens wrote and read and lectured like a bald fiend, pausing to puke between speaking engagements. This was not fighting cancer, but fighting for dignity and purpose in the face of it. An atheist to the end, to my mind he was nevertheless enacting spirit, what is beyond the body's story.

Somehow not yet dead
at the end of my journey—
this autumn's evening
        —Basho

So it turned out Kea, like me, was mortally ill. She had an adrenal disease. That's why, for a young dog, she was so low key. Once, though, Kea's wild nature enacted itself on a forest hike near our house. Suddenly she bolted, disappeared into tall grass, and then a wild piglet began squealing. I screamed for Kea, terrified an angry sow's attack was imminent. But no sow appeared, only Kea from the underbrush, a black piglet clamped in her jaws, thrashing it back and forth until it went lank. And then her predator instinct broke, and gentleness returned. She dropped the piglet and trotted to me. I recoiled. What kind of animal *was* she? I never saw her kill again, but I never saw her the same way, either.

This is not a war story. This is not a romantic comedy, though at times it feels like theater of the absurd. As in, when at the café in Seattle where Mara and I stopped to get lunch after the procedure to draw fluid out of my abdomen, the waiter poured our water and asked, "How can I help you today?"

And I said, "Seriously? Do you really mean that? Are you sure you want to know?" And he, taken aback, laughed nervously and took our order. He avoided us after that.

"Can you get me some opium, a match, and a pipe?"

"Can you explain suffering?"

"Is there any hope on the menu?"

> *hopeful things: two eggs*
> *on greens the waiter brings poached*
> *perfect: her palm on my cheek*

I'm getting ahead of myself. I don't want to write (or live) a story about being a cancer patient. I don't want to write (or live) a story about battling cancer to the bitter, bitter end. I don't want to be bitter. I don't want to claim that cancer has made me a better, stronger person, that it's a gift, that it's an enemy. I don't want to write (or live) a tragedy. I don't want to write a cancer rant about all of the emails, letters, and packages I've received in response to published essays in which I reveal my cancer diagnosis: emails, letters, and packages from strangers offering me the chance at salvation—some by way of religion, some by way of marijuana oil, breast milk, coffee enemas, or saltwater springs—before it's too late. I don't want to rage, even though rage is what I felt the other day at the sight of well-dressed groups of youth on the Seattle streets handing out pamphlets entitled "The True Story of Jesus." Rage is what fed my unholy desire to scream into the face of a young man holding a hand-lettered sign declaring, "God loves and cares about you." Even though I don't disbelieve it. Because I couldn't get the image of the little bald girl out of my mind. Though I am a poet, and I abide by Keats's idea of "negative capability," the ability to hold two opposing things in the mind at once, I couldn't do it. I couldn't hold the image of the little bald girl in the wheelchair and the image of the young man's sign in my mind, much less in my heart, at once.

I carry into yoga this new grief for Kea like a sparked flint. Practice starts off slowly, and before I can bypass my mind, get into my breathing and body, they arise within me, other griefs outside myself. The young moose stabbed to death by three men in Anchorage. The artist in town whose eighteen-year-old son died suddenly two weeks ago. The unarmed black man killed by police in Baltimore. The five thousand and counting killed in the Nepal earthquake. *The ritual begins now.*

How do I begin it when I don't know who or what God is or what kind of mercy he/she/it bestows or doesn't bestow, or to understand the nature of his/her/its love? Yet in my own way I am a believer. In wild nature life and death in all their variations make some kind of sense. In my human body's solidarity with other life forms, all of us are mortal. I believe in that. I believe in love as well. Out of my Catholic upbringing I carried a simple math that stayed with me through all my spiritual wanderings: Love = Divinity.

Weather-beaten bones
I'll leave your heart exposed
to cold, piercing winds
                                    —Basho

I think of it now as "the parable of the calf." Kea was with me the winter day my friend and I found the calf, a day of alternating sun and hard rain, the gray low clouds pouring west. An ocean swell rumbled continuously, with a breathing thrum, a cycling like an engine.

In rain jackets, we hiked slowly, winding our way through cow pastures overgrown with invasive lantana and Christmas berry that scratched our legs. A fence line ran parallel to the edge of the earth, a hundred-foot buffer between pasture and cliffs falling steeply to the surging ocean. Pono Van Holt's herd of beef cows grazed near the fence line, which we crossed by slithering beneath electrified wire. It was calving time, and mothers and young hid in tall grass apart from the rest, some outside the fence, in the ironwood break along the sea cliffs. The sun sank; the light between rain squalls was stark. We talked and stopped for my friend to collect hallucinogenic mushrooms, which she dropped into a white paper bag, like a hippie form of takeout—tiny conical caps on long thin stems growing out of cow pies, staining blue when broken. I had read that winter an article by Michael Pollan describing clinical experiments in which guided magic mushroom trips erased fear of death in people with terminal illnesses. My friend used the mushrooms as part of her healing practice. Our search slowed us down even more, kept our eyes to the earth.

The streets of Seattle offer their own sermons and parables. All of them yesterday made a similar point: in suffering, in pain, no one is alone, though we often feel, even on thronged sidewalks, isolated. We see fellow sufferers as "other" when their brand of suffering doesn't resemble our own. Visible pain is easy to find in Seattle, side by side with hipsterish youth and youthful hipsterism, optimism, wealth, designer coffee and kombucha, lumberjack beards, and trendy rumpled retro tweed. Much of the city is undergoing gentrification. Police clear sidewalks of the homeless, vacant lots of dealers. Mental health services in Washington are poorly funded, and psychologically ill people are often released onto the streets. But some stories, the ones that become parables, defy easy explanation. I'm thinking of the relatively kempt Asian man carefully laid out upon the sidewalk close to a brick wall, his backpack deliberately placed near his head, his arm around it, his glasses removed and folded there between his head and the wall, his decent clothes and shoes and haircut giving us pause—what was going on here? He was sleeping, dead to the living world flowing past him. Yet perhaps a little concerned, even in his public display of private sorrow, even in his exposure and lack of privacy, with appearances, with order, with dignity.

> On the bank of the Fuji River, we came upon an abandoned child, about age two, its sobs stirring our pity. The child's parents must have been crushed by the waves of this floating world to have left him here beside the rushing river to pass like dew.
>
> —Basho

Just past the main cattle herd, just past a north-south fence line, we saw in the ironwoods near the cliffs a lone calf, mostly cream colored, something strange in its stance, back end much higher than front, moving in a jerking fashion. As we crept closer, we saw that it was hobbling on deformed or broken forelegs. They folded under at the ankles. The calf managed a few steps on its ankles, then lay down.

My horror morphed into panic. "We have to do something," I cried to my friend. Someone had to come and kill the calf, save it from a miserable, lonely death. My friend, caught up in my angst, suggested carrying the calf back home, but that would have been physically impossible, and stupid. So we crept forward, low to the ground. The calf seemed not at all distressed, didn't make a sound. She wasn't a newborn; her coat was dry. She wasn't emaciated. She rested her chin on the ground. Her brown eyes peered at us from the flat of her skull. Black flies speckled her cream coat. Her pushed-in snout was wet in a bovine way. Other than being alone and crippled and tired, she seemed oddly healthy and placid. We decided the only sane thing was to call Pono, the cattleman, apparently a good person. Nearby, a flock of white egrets dropped out of the sky to roost in a dead tree. The herd of cows moaned, grazing farther up the slope. We called Pono. We walked away. We resumed our conversation.

> High over wild seas
> surrounding Sado Island—
> the River of Heaven
> > —Basho

I'm trying to wring some meaning out of what feels sometimes like a story that can't have a happy ending—for me, for Basho's abandoned child, for the calf. It's some consolation that even Basho—who underwent "arduous studies in poetry, Buddhism, history, Taoism, Confucianism, Shintoism, and some very important Zen training" (according to one of his translators, Sam Hamill)—had little insight to offer readers into the fact of the abandoned child.

How can this happen? Did his father despise him? Did his mother neglect him? I think not. This must be the will of heaven. We mourn his fate.

Even Basho recorded no heroic story.

I left him what food I could.

A cancer story is certainly no more heroic than the story of that man sleeping with something I can only call dignity on Pine Street in the middle of the day. I didn't choose my fate. My efforts at survival are almost purely selfish. Almost. I don't want others to suffer on my behalf. I said as much to my brother-in-law the other day, in a fit of self-pity, and he vehemently protested, "We want to go through this with you!" On its surface this sounds foolish, like saying to myself, "I want to find more creatures dying and alone on my walks." Yet when the worst things happen to others, we choose to go through it with them, and in that we are brave. So maybe this is a love story in the end. To be sick isn't brave, but to love and remain beside someone in sickness is brave and perhaps even divine. Knowing what we know about loss.

What does it mean that Nietzsche reportedly went insane near the end of his life after watching a horse being beaten? In that moment in the pasture, I felt myself go momentarily insane with the cruelty of the calf's fate. I fell into radical helplessness and projection. I forgot prayer. I forgot ritual. I forgot mystery. I forgot *bearing witness.* I forgot *bearing.* It's very like the falling into chemotherapy's malaise during the week after an infusion, believing there is only this. It's hard to connect with spirit when the broken, suffering body—mine, another's—gets in the way. In the days that followed the encounter with the calf, I tried to make sense of it but couldn't. I was focused on the wrong impulse. So great was my hunger to understand. So great was my desire, my hope—that the calf's existence had meaning. So great was my rejection of meaninglessness, of an indifferent universe, of senseless suffering.

> *The whole country devastated*
> *Only mountains and rivers remain.*
> *In springtime, at the ruined castle,*
> *The grass is always green.*
> —Tu Fu

A scholar of religion and the environment, Mary Evelyn Tucker believes humankind stands right now on the brink of transformation, if only we would absorb all of the new knowledge of how the universe was born. That knowledge, she thinks, is so mind-blowing it has the power to change the way we as a species see ourselves. From her collaboration with the cosmologist Brian Swimme, she concludes that the ongoing creative ritual that is the universe began with "a roaring force from one unknowable moment, this origin moment." In the beginning, she says, was "a great roaring forth." When I read these words for the first time, I absorb them bodily, as sound, as though they'd opened a door to a blast furnace in my head. In the beginning, not the Word, but the roar. "From the creative processes of galaxies and stars and finally planetary systems over 10 billion years, our sun, our Earth, our moon emerged, and eventually humans were born." This sounds gentle, and well modulated, the way it's laid out in her sentence. Yet her words fill me with what's perhaps meant by "the fear of God." Our evolution doesn't begin with first life, but much further back—with roaring. Tucker's speaking of this is hopeful, ebullient, awed. But what I hear is different. Out of the roaring comes something we call a bog orchid, and something we call *Orcinus orca*, and something we call creek, and something we call lightning-struck tree, and something we call aurora, and something we call howling infant, and something we call cancer.

A cancer story is not a God story in the usual way, not a story about answered prayers or miracles in any conventional sense. Which is not to say I don't take comfort from loved ones saying "I'm praying for you." Which is not to say I don't pray for myself and others. A cancer story is a God story, I see now, in the sense of that roaring. I don't really understand anything else, how it works, or why. I will never find the meaning in that calf's crippled legs, or in the child's being stricken with incurable cancer. But it helps me to think, "Out of roaring we came." Life is not gentle, but ferocious. "With your fierce tears, I pray," wrote Dylan Thomas in his most famous poem "Do Not Go Gentle into That Good Night," about his father's dying. One day last week, I walked down the streets of Seattle, amid the beggars and ravers and homeless teens with their open guitar cases, the dealers and the insane, and in my head I pleaded, *Please, God, help me, take this away from me,* and help came to me in human form, as a young man playing his mandolin beside me on the ferry that evening. He pressed his song into my begging hand.

I was raised Catholic. Once, in a strange ceremony sprung upon our unsuspecting afterschool religion class, I was even "saved" by a sect of "charismatics" that had formed in our church. As a child I read the Bible and kept up a personal relationship to Jesus, who felt like an actual friend. I prayed. I went to confession. I experienced forgiveness. Yet I don't know the "true" story of Jesus. In college, I gradually shed the Catholic faith, yet I clung to certain tenets. I know that Jesus was incarnate, a human, and he suffered, and I believe he heard the roaring of creation in his ears. I know that when he pleaded with God, not as his God, but as his father, when he pleaded for mercy, it wasn't given. His father watched it happen, the crucifixion, and did nothing to stop it. Jesus said, *Thy will be done,* and maybe it was, and what that says about that particular God, who is also supposed to be a father, I'm afraid to think about too hard. When I rail, it's that notion of God I rage against.

The ritual begins now.

When I jolted awake at 4:00 a.m. the night after we encountered the calf, it was the calf that woke me, along with the curtain of rain lashing the house and, I knew, lashing the ironwood grove where she lay. I prayed that night. *Oh please, some fucking mercy.* I prayed the words of Cyrus Cassels's poem "Soul Make a Path through Shouting," lodged in my head since I read them, *Make this earth a heaven.* I offered up the only thing I could, that prayer, this memory, this attempt to fashion it into a story, to hold it in my consciousness, to pass it along. So that she might have dignity, I want to say, but I don't hold that power. She *is* dignity, with or without anyone's prayer, with or without anyone's witnessing— her calm in the face of her fate, her gentleness in the face of the roaring. The broken, tender fact of her.

Hearing the monkey's cries—
what of the child abandoned
to the autumn wind?
     —Basho

I will stake my life on the story of the calf, even if I don't know what it means, even if it is a Zen koan I'm far too uneducated and unpracticed to unravel. Even if I carry it to my own end. Because putting them together—the plodding pedestrian drama of my cancer, and the mystery, the question of the calf, and the five-hundred-year-old question of Basho's abandoned child, and the mystery of the origins of this creative, roaring universe continuously making itself—I see there's no choice. Our stories are not to spin one way or another. The ritual begins when we gather our stories and place them side by side, even when they refuse to resolve. A cancer story by itself is one-way, time-bound. A story of life on a mortal earth is told in the round. The writer Kathleen Norris says, "Existence is not a puzzle to be solved but a narrative to be inherited and undergone and transformed person by person."

Outside the windows of the yoga studio, the air is alive with birdsong, a relentless, ferocious urgency of nest building, egg laying, young raising, hatchling squabbling. As the bodies inside the log building enact a round, from opening breath to closing corpse pose, the earth enacts an unceasing cycling, casts its unwavering eye. By July, the birds—territories established, nests built, eggs laid and hatched—will fall silent. Suffering and mercy continuously enacted, the trajectory unmerciful—death eating away at a body—human, canine, avian, fern—even the body of a child.

Both mercy and the unmerciful have come to me by way of earthly hands and earthly phenomena, always changing, being born and dying away. Out of the roaring they come, equally. Mercy comes by way of cumulous building and darkening now over the bluff and releasing rain onto the dry woods. By way of a shy animal named Kea who walked with me for a time. By way of my sister's palm on my face. And if those are God's hands, as some song says, then they are God-flesh and God-bone, God-stem and God-feather, God-paws and God-rain. As well as God-death, and God-suffering. In the common plea for mercy, we're not alone. The homeless of Seattle, the cancer sufferers at the hospital, Jesus in the garden of Gethsemane and on the cross, the abandoned calf and the abandoned child, all are one and the same. That is the truth I know about Jesus, but I don't know what it means.

Becoming Body

On a branch
floating downriver,
a cricket is singing.
    —Kobayashi Issa (tr. Jane Hirshfield)

I'M WRITING TO THE SOUND of running water—a stream thick with eroded dirt from miles of travel through a gulch cut into the side of an extinct volcano. At the edge of the land in Hawaii, where my husband and I spend a few months each winter, you can hike to a vantage in the ironwood trees to glimpse, through jungley vegetation, brown water pouring from a lava tube at the top of the gulch and plunging fifty feet to a pool before heading seaward. The stream is ephemeral, but this winter it's been flowing for more than a month, since the first big rains. It courses through the gulch and spills into the ocean, sending a murk-plume into the turquoise and white wash of swells breaking in the cove.

I am here for grounding, and the most grounding sound for me is fresh water rushing over and around stones, shallow water's throaty vocalizations. It's how I'm rooted, having grown up at the confluence of creeks, Silver and Walnut, in western New York—having waded in and skated upon and hiked up and down those creeks all of my childhood. I'm sitting on a tablecloth beside the stream. When I get hot, I can dip my bare feet into the water. When I look at my computer screen, I see my reflection and take a photograph of the phenomenon: my head eerily ghosting a page of text, my baldness hidden by a scarf. I've been inhabiting a body without hair for six months now. For two years, I have been living with terminal breast cancer.

One of the things I love about this shady spot under a bonsai-shaped ironwood is the way the salt-loving shrub *naupaka* bobs in the current where it runs along the stream's opposite bank. In the midst of so much alien flora, native naupaka thrives, spills down the slope, fleshy leaves tugged by the stream's flow. I want to say *the way it's always been*, but I know that's false. This island is young, geologically speaking, emerging from the ocean as an uninhabitable, hot, swelling dome of lava less than a half million years ago. Through ongoing volcanic eruption on the other side of the island, it's still being created. Only in my imagination is there a *way it's always been*.

Pinao—dragonflies—arrive to hover, then vanish. Overhead, piping and keening, two *kolea*—Pacific golden plovers—arrow toward the headland. Like me, plovers migrate here each winter from Alaska, thirty-five hundred miles they cover in three days. This same pair probably returns to this gulch each winter of their lives.

I keep getting distracted from the story I'm about to tell by everything going about its business around me. I'm mesmerized by water pillowing over a stone, forming a burbling eddy below it. I'm startled by the booming of swells in the cove.

The story I'm about to tell made me feel small. It's a story about baldness. Though I wear my headscarf a lot less than I used to in private, I admit at the beginning to having felt self-conscious of my baldness even with my husband, who has known me for thirty years. Craig dreaded my loss of hair. It reminded him of the first time it fell out, five years ago, when I was diagnosed with early-stage breast cancer; when cancer, for eight months, devoured our lives. It's a brutal treatment, an attempt at complete eradication of the disease, which in my case failed. What failed for Craig was his dogged belief that once treatment ended, once my hair grew back, we'd resume the lives cancer had interrupted. All that summer of my first chemo, I'd lived with my sister near Boston, and he'd doggedly planted our garden in Alaska, filled our freezer with fish for winter, and carried on our research work, even when it meant I underwent chunks of the ordeal without him. He kept the backdrop of our lives intact, as though it were a painting and I a figure temporarily missing. As though I could, when treatment ended, slip back into the picture without changing it. When my hair fell out this time, cancer was no longer an interruption in our lives, it was a defining feature.

A bald head is cancer's mark, but what it is, actually, is chemo's mark, the mark of drugs, like yew tree–derived Taxol and mustard gas–derived Cytoxan, that kill cancer and all fast-growing cells in the body, those forming the body's protective barriers—hair, skin, membranes, nerves. A bald head is a mark of vulnerability. It's the mark of the lengths we go through to survive.

By now, I have lost my eyelashes and eyebrows too; this gives my eyes a vulnerable yet craggy look. Browlessness emphasizes the bony ridge protruding slightly where my eyebrows used to be. I admit to studying myself daily in the mirror, wondering things. Do I look older? (Last time I lost my hair, people mistook me, twice, for my sister's mother.) Does baldness render my gender ambivalent? Does it make me look hipster-androgynous? Does it un-sex me? Does it make me look chic, with my "nicely shaped head," as some people insist? Go ahead, say it, does it make me look (the least original, not to mention misplaced, thing you can say to a chemo-bald person) like Sinead O'Connor? (Or like an elf, as one person insisted. Ask yourself, honestly, do you want to look like a hairless elf?) A bald woman without eyebrows or eyelashes does not look like Sinead O'Connor. She looks like she has cancer. Try it on your own face. (Clearly baldness makes me snarky. A friend asked me, "What if some people who say you look beautiful bald are telling you the truth?" No comment.)

And it's only hair, right? Worth losing to save (or prolong) your life. There's a lot at stake with cancer, the least of which—right?—is hair. Then why is it one of breast cancer's most profound griefs? There's even research to confirm this. I'm no cultural anthropologist when it comes to hair. I can only offer my own observations of its power. In the waiting area of the oncology unit where I was first treated, a glass case displayed a bird's nest woven from a woman's hair. An accompanying text told the story: how, grief-struck, this woman collected her fallen hair from the shower drain and sprinkled it around her yard. How the next year, her husband found the nest. The nest and its story and its grief act as counterpoint to the story you'll hear in the examining rooms or in the chemo ward. If you're getting chemotherapy with "curative" intent (rather than palliative, or symptom-managing, or the hope of life-prolonging intent, as I am), nurses are likely to say, "The good news is, your hair will grow back!" They don't say it will grow back unrecognizably, often gray or (in my case, three years ago) pure white; that it will grow back curly when it was straight, straight when it was curly. They like to say it helps to shave your head preemptively, to save yourself the trauma of those clumps clogging the shower drain. They don't mention the nest, or suggest a way to transform your coming losses.

What is it about hair? What is it about hair and the body and the sense of self? The body: it's only flesh, bone, blood, the tangible aspects of who we are. Hair: it's only dead matter. Yet we meet the world via the body. And the world responds. And we listen. A long time ago, when I was a teenager, a teacher fixed his gaze and his language on my breasts, and it caused me to curl my shoulders inward, something I still do. When I inhabit that pose, one friend calls me a cormorant. A long time ago, dipping our naked bodies into a muskeg pond, another friend said I looked like Helga in the Wyeth paintings. Wyeth's model was earthy, curvaceous, and my friend who made the comparison, tiny, fragile; I saw myself and my peasant body differently after that. A long time ago, a man asked if he could bury his face in my long hair. A long time ago, when I cut my long hair short, several male friends expressed shock and dismay. Not long ago, Craig came up behind me as I sat, bareheaded, writing at my desk, nuzzled my neck, said, "Thank you for making the bed." My self-consciousness around him eased up after that.

It's suddenly cloudy. I look up the slope to the top of the gulch where legend has it there's a buried locomotive from the sugar cane days. In this gulch, an older legend has it, King Kamehameha was hidden as a child when prophesies that he'd unite the Hawaiian Islands circulated among his enemies. I've learned to question romantic notions about this place (and about cancer), but true or false, these stories color the way I experience being here. My own story is that I imagine I'm not the only woman who's sat on this bank, listening to this stream, coming here for some sort of solace or relief from the heat or her relentless toil, her day spent laboring in the sugar cane fields. As if manifesting this dream, a Brazilian cardinal lands on the opposite bank and splashes a little water on her face. Hundreds of years ago, that woman would have been Hawaiian, but in the last century, Chinese, Japanese, Portuguese, Korean, or Filipina, one of the immigrants brought to this place to work the sugar cane plantations, wave after wave, the owners ever on the quest for a cheap, docile labor force. Someone, perhaps, brought a body of illness to this place. Perhaps this stream, originating high on the mountain, was known for healing, or at least for sustenance. Surely, somewhere in this gulch, people grew taro, a starchy staple of Polynesian culture, long before the time of sugar cane and missionaries and cattle. Even now, a massive feral taro plant grows along the stream's upper parts.

We found that plant, a friend and I, the other day. We were sitting each upon our own smooth boulder in the stream, and she was telling me she was leaving her husband. Once, she said, someone dreamed about building a Buddhist monastery in the gulch. She used to visit the spot where we sat with her husband on hot days to lie in the water, and they imagined saffron-robed monks filing by along the stream in silence, practicing walking meditation. This scene planted itself in my mind so vividly, it feels like my own memory, another myth woven from the sound of water, its wet clay scent, and the play of light filtered through the *kukui* nut trees. She told me about a spot she used to visit for solace on another part of the island, years ago, a stand of old kukui trees in the midst of a barren landscape of recent lava flows—a green refuge known as a *kipuka*. Native Hawaiians say a kipuka is "an oasis saved from Pele's embrace"; Pele being the volcano goddess, the goddess of fire. Poet Pattiann Rogers defines it also as "a safe time and place where one perceives things clearly."

Yesterday, deep into my cancer story, far from any notion of kipuka, rooted in my cancer-self, my sense of urgency overtaking all else, I walked into Craig's office, where he was working at his computer, and I said, "We have to go. Now. To Waimea. I have to get my blood counts checked, to see how anemic I am, to see if I need a transfusion before my next chemo."

Craig looked up from his screen, told me he was in the middle of something, and could I wait. He sounded annoyed, then petulant. He said our friend Karl was coming down with his wood chipper and now he would have to call Karl and tell him not to come. And the trimmed mess of branches in our driveway would have to sit there for another day.

Here's where my protective sister, my unwavering defender, would say, "What an ass. You've got fucking cancer!" Here's where I'd say it to myself. There are many enduring myths that form around cancer, and they are destructive. If you get cancer, and you have a caregiver, and if you believe, for example, in the myth of Noble Caregiver, you'll be disappointed. Each ill person internalizes some variation of this story as a litany of "shoulds." In my own mythic narrative, Craig jumps up from his swivel chair and says, "Great, what can I do?" He's gung-ho to help; he's uber-positive. That's him, Cancer Guy. He's your man. He rises, briskly, cheerfully, to every one of cancer's occasions. Or he stands at the ready with a cool washcloth and an empathic expression and a bottle of anti-nausea meds.

That's not my man. Craig *does* rise to every cancer occasion, but he doesn't always do it instantly or willingly or cheerfully. He lurches into position. And his position is often awkward, one foot in regular life, one foot in cancer-caregiver world. He still sees his role as maintaining normalcy in his life and mine—especially in regards to those things we both love, those things that brought us together. Which is to say—maintaining control. He times our research trips around my chemo infusions so I can still work with him on the boat. He fishes and grows gardens so I can eat clean food. In waiting rooms, at the infusion center, there he is, sitting beside me, his laptop perched on his knees, his cell phone pressed to his ear, working on a grant proposal. I have to interrupt him when the bag of Taxol arrives. He indulges me when I ask him to place his hands on the bag with mine, to burn our desire into the poisonous fluid: *Kill those motherfuckers.* Sometimes, he Skypes into my oncology appointments, and my sister and I place my phone, his face grainy on the screen, on its own chair.

When I get my cancer-mind out of my ass, I remember that Craig needs time to adjust to sudden, hitherto unannounced, changes to his day's plans; he always has. I remember that when Craig first heard the news of my cancer, he lit candles and prayed. I remember that when Craig heard the news of my cancer's return, he wept, then helped me drag quilts and pillows outside. He lay down with me on the cold ground. We wrapped our bodies around each other and slept.

Cancer has made no saint of Craig, nor of me. We fight, we nag, we annoy one another. Once in a rage, I flung a broom across the kitchen table, barely missing his head, and after a beat, we laughed. We know one look will break us down, one of us will begin to smile, and that will be that. I know these things. But yesterday, first, I rose to the occasion of Craig's annoyance. I rose to the occasion of my desire for Noble Cancer Man. I argued that I did tell him, more than once, that we'd be driving to Waimea this week for a blood test. He just didn't listen. The blah-blah-blah, unheroic, mundane, back-and-forth volley between Cancer

Man, stomping around, suddenly needing to fry himself an egg, and Cancer Woman, bald and aggrieved. Leaving in a huff. Driving to the hospital in Waimea by herself, Goddammit. That's what I did.

Driving up the mountain road, I turned on public radio, and the BBC was broadcasting from the other side of the planet a story about the murders, rapes, and disappearances of indigenous women in Canada. A young activist described the racism rampant against First Nations people in that country, as an interviewer cross-examined him: *Really? Really? Don't you think "atrocity" is a strong word to use?* A young woman, her utterances broken, recounted her rape at a protest rally. A family grieved for a missing daughter.

Recollecting the news story now, as I look around me, everything feels fragile—the plovers facing those twice-a-year thirty-five-hundred-mile nonstop migrations, flying at twenty thousand feet and a hundred miles per hour; the stream, ephemeral due to diversion of water for agriculture in the higher elevations; the native vegetation surrounded by encroaching ironwood, threatened like every other endemic species by invasive weeds; my relationship with Craig; my identity; my hold on this earth; my hold on this body; the vulnerability of women's bodies, everywhere. It seems, suddenly, astounding—our ability to fight, to forget, to fall asleep, to wake, to forge on, to make plans for another and another day.

Twenty minutes into my drive, Craig called (as he always does) and apologized (as he always does) for reacting badly (which he sometimes does). I forgave him and said I loved him, said I was sorry too, but I still felt the crater of grief inside me, until stress displaced it. I realized I hadn't been watching my speed. A vehicle had been tailgating me, a big Ford truck, unable to pass on the narrow, winding road. My rage flooded back, displacing both grief and stress. I refused to pull over and let the truck by. My rage had nothing to do with Craig, nothing to do with the tailgater. My acupuncturist says cancer is fire and chemo is fire; using chemo to fight cancer is fighting fire with fire. A friend of mine, who's had breast cancer twice, told me rage is fire. Held inside, she said, it feeds cancer. She told me to go deep into the woods and scream it out. But to me, rage is water, an aquifer pooled too deep to fully apprehend, until it violently upwells. It's water too vast to be specific only to my individual pain. On the island of Hawaii, the closest equivalent is Kilauea volcano, its latest eruption driving people from their homes, burning up acres of forest, oozing across roads, utterly unpredictable in its movements. This winter, the creeping, burning lava has caused the evacuation of an entire town. The goddess of the volcano is Pele, who destroys as she creates, who is known for her rage and vengeance at injustice. The urban legend goes that the price for removing even one chunk of her body from the island is such bad luck that the post offices are filled with mailed-back lava rocks.

In the hospital, agitated, I sat cross-legged in the blue infusion room recliner, texting my sister, waiting for my blood count results to tell me if I needed a transfusion.

I told my sister that a gentle-looking lab tech had walked in to ask me for yet another tube of blood, saying, "Good afternoon, sir." I had looked over at him, startled, and he'd realized his mistake. "Sorry," he'd said, "I mean 'ma'am.'"

There are moments in cancer world when the divide between the healthy and the unhealthy is particularly felt, when we do seem, in Susan Sontag's famous metaphor, to inhabit separate kingdoms, the kingdom of the well and the kingdom of the sick. When you're pushing an IV stand. When you're tethered to a pump. When you're clad in a hospital johnny. When you're bald and someone out in the world reminds you of it, you realize your private travail is impossible to hide. The realm of cancer is its own ecosystem. As a friend says, cancer "lights people up," lights up their fears. Cancer, like a volcano, is so dread a force, it expresses itself in the culture first as metaphor, then as cliché. The Watergate scandal, for example, was described by John Dean as "a cancer within—close to the Presidency—that's growing." Cancer in our cultural consciousness stands for boundless evil: Islamic extremism, drug violence in Mexico, Sharia law tribunals, clergy sex abuse, soccer match-fixing, the national debt, mortgage scandals. All these have been labeled cancers. Cancer, ultimately, means suffering, means death, and what lights people up more than that, causes them to turn away? Yet for me, the outward symbol of cancer, baldness, is at times a strange attractant. In a coffee shop the other day, I sat talking with friends and a woman spotted me, swooped in, and whispered into my ear, "Are you a survivor?" I've had acquaintances ask me in a clothing store if I'd had a mastectomy, a woman fitting me for glasses ask me for my prognosis, a stranger at the beach say, "You must be living each day to the fullest," another ask me if I was bald "on purpose," and when I said no, tell me about a machine that could cure cancer. In each encounter my illusion of a private identity, of control over that identity, shattered.

I joked to my sister about being called "sir," but I swear, when I studied the selfie I texted to her, of my face looking down at the camera above the part-full saline syringe left dangling from my port, I saw it: not exactly manliness, but absence. No bangs to soften the angles of my face. No lashes to decorate my eyes, no eyebrows to raise in irony. Lit by hospital fluorescents, my face looked tired, depleted of color, unguarded.

So I should have been relieved to learn I wasn't anemic enough for a blood transfusion. I should have been relieved to walk out of that place, but I felt unmoored, unable to shake a sense of exposure. In the health food store afterward, I felt hyperaware of my cancer identity. I avoided eye contact as I wove my way through the narrow aisles. In the checkout line, I felt the gaze of the woman next to me. I could see her regarding me from my peripheral vision (or she seemed to be regarding me, I hold no trust in my judgment)—Rattled Cancer Woman buying not kale, but two bags of coffee beans and a package of cookies.

In the car, I switched on the radio, this time to a BBC story about discrimination against Muslim citizens in France. A mother described how she was not allowed to attend her daughter's school trips as a chaperone because she wears a hijab. When she drops her off at school, the mother takes her daughter's headscarf off, sending her naked into the world. How it must feel to let her child go, hair exposed, shed of an identity. Hair so powerful in her culture it must be concealed.

I am making too much of this, I know. I know it now; I knew it then. But I kept repeating the story—to Craig, to our friends. I kept texting wisecracks to my sister. I put on Craig's button-down cotton shirt (which makes me look utterly flat-chested) and his baseball cap and posed for the camera and texted it to her.

This morning, someone posted a video on Facebook of two young women salsa dancing. They were sexy, completely inhabiting their bodies, synchronous to each other and to the music. Why did it knock the wind out of me? Why did it drive me, ultimately, down here alone to the stream? I've never inhabited my body in that way; I'm a self-conscious dancer. I'm not nostalgic for my twenties. I'm fifty-one, and I like my age. Aging, for me, is (should be) a privilege. Before I saw the video clip, I felt again the incident of being called "sir," relegating it to the junk drawer—my collection of weird cancer anecdotes. I can't say if those young salsa-dancing women were aware of their bodies in that moment, if they were self-conscious. I'm nostalgic not for their bodies, but for their relationship to their bodies, for their using their bodies to communicate to each other and to watchers, their bodies saying something people want to hear.

During my first round of chemo in 2010, then as now, I went to water for solace. Almost daily when I was able, I walked three miles around a pond. Afterward I'd find a hidden spot shaded by pines. One day, a pair of teenaged girls, blonde and bikini-clad, breasts-down on their boogie boards, made landfall on a nearby patch of sand. They stayed, talking, for most of an hour. They didn't see me. I couldn't take my eyes away, trying to describe in my journal the swale at the nape of their backs, the smooth dune of their skin. I felt like a sack of chemotherapy. At home, I studied my reflection in the outdoor shower mirror. My body was a map to my new identity, yet I couldn't decipher it. It was a map without legend. Nonetheless, I examined my bald head, my mastectomy scar. I'd turn one way and see a middle-aged woman, the other way and see a ten-year-old girl.

I've decided to relocate to a spot along the rocky beach. I walk to an eroded bank and find a patch of shade under overhanging naupaka shrubs, but still, it's hot. I look over my shoulder to make sure I'm alone. (Why? No one ever comes here but me.) Only then do I pull off my headscarf and sit cross-legged in the shade and let the wind cool my bare skin. I open my computer and notice again my reflection on the screen, my bald head wavering behind my words.

I write for a time, but the heat drives me down the lava rocks to a tide pool. Crouching on a boulder, I peer around for lurking morays, and then cup my hand and scoop water to pour over my scalp. I let water runnel down my arms. Cooled off now, I watch zebra blennies camouflaged by sand. Two whelk shells slide along the bottom, co-opted by tiny orange hermit crabs with iridescent bands of blue across their faces. *Ha uke uke*, endemic invertebrates that look like purple pincushions, slip down rocks inch by inch. I lose my thoughts watching all of this, only regain awareness when the hot sun drives me to pour another palmful of water over my head.

Am I baptizing myself? Into what faith? I feel the wind play across the sensitive skin over my skull, the heat inside me dissipate. Though I have faith in science to explain many things, including the biology of my cancer, it's not enough for this. My sense of loss—my grief—over my baldness is dense, and like my rage in the car, inexplicable.

In a medical journal I found online, in a study on the psychological impact of baldness on patients, the authors call it "a form of disfigurement that can affect a person's sense of self and identity." Hair loss, according to another study, has a greater psychological impact on women with breast cancer than loss of a breast. It's impossible not to absorb the words *a form of disfigurement*, though everyone in my life would argue against it. And if you google "chemo baldness," you'll find plenty of photos of bald women who look chic, sexy, hip. But look closely: all of them have eyebrows. The women without eyebrows look vulnerable—they look like they have cancer. I look like I have cancer. I have cancer, which is anything but sexy, despite the title of a book someone sent me once called *Crazy Sexy Cancer*. A book I flung across the room. My headscarf hides nothing. So what—who—is my headscarf protecting? When I'm in yoga and it slips up above my ears, I pull it down, though it conceals not the fact of my baldness, just my actual baldness. Why am I protecting others from the mark of cancer on my body? Why am I so ashamed?

Here, the breeze on my head at this moment, the tickle of ironwood needles along my ear, is actually sensuous. Here, where no one's watching, and most importantly, for a few moments at a time, *I'm* not watching, I am simply a being among other beings, each strange in its way: scaly, finned, winged, feathered, with or without bones, two- or four- or six- or eight-legged, or without legs, like the pair of humpback whales who just now dove off the headland.

All day, here beside water, I've been trying to find my way to the opposite of the word *disfigure*. I've been trying to find my way out of a story of being called "sir." It's said transformation happens by fire. Sometimes isolation is essential to transformation. Sometimes isolation is a form of refuge—the only protection against enormous forces of change. The high elevations of this island's volcanoes are a refuge for native birds; up there, cold protects them from disease-carrying mosquitoes. A refuge is sometimes invisible: it's what's buried, dormant, under what appears razed, denuded. It's seeds. Under the tens of thousands of acres of cow pasture along the mountain road to Waimea, under the invasive grasses, exists a seed bank—the earth's capacity to heal. If you fence out the cows and feral pigs and goats, the native forest begins to grow back all on its own. Sometimes a refuge is turbulent: in solitude, we wrestle our angels, our demons. Sociologist, author, and cancer survivor Arthur Frank puts it this way: "The holiness of the ground is created in the wrestling that sanctifies the ground."

Like the cricket floating by on its branch in Issa's poem, carried toward an uncertain outcome, what I'm about to claim as refuge is a temporary state. That's all I can hope for. Here in the gulch I find refuge. Where my baldness means nothing. Where my disfigured body is holy. This place, the gulch where I've been wandering bareheaded, where I've watched crabs with and without shells in the tide pools and camouflaged zebra blennies and purple *ha uke uke*, where I've written all afternoon on the stream bank with my feet in the water is kipuka—a green oasis saved, just for today, from Pele's fire.

The Equality of Flesh and Absence

THE HOLES STARTED WITH DOGS. Then cats, then curlews, then brothers, then aspects of self. They started with Serry, the half wolf/half Siberian husky, half brown-eyed/half blue-eyed animal we had no business keeping in suburbia. Even with our two acres of backyard, he was restless, so my father chained him. Serry chewed through his leather collars and next thing we knew the police were calling to report he'd treed or mauled or outright killed somebody's cat. The first time he disappeared for longer than a day, he dragged himself home on three legs. A bullet wound in a back leg wept blood. A vet used a metal pin to fix the bone. The next time he disappeared, it was forever. Rumor had it the farmer down the road shot him. That was the first one, the hole left by Serry. His killing sprees and wildness made no sense to me, a five-year-old girl who sat astride his back and let him lick her face. My father's beating him with a chain as punishment for his escapes and depredations didn't make sense to me either. My love for him was unbound by any distinction between human and animal, and when he didn't come back, I grieved hard.

Which is what I'm doing today, grieving for an animal. Craig and I are anchored up in Squire Cove, hiding out from the equinox storm, which is a mid-September phenomenon here, announcing summer's violent and unequivocal end on Alaska's north gulf coast. In 2011 the equinox storm was strong enough to be dubbed a hurricane, with sustained wind speeds of sixty-five knots. I marked the lowest dip of the needle on our barometer in permanent ink: 964. This morning, it's fallen to 975. Gusts zigzag across the bay, drive sheets of rain sideways before them, slamming against the boat, shrieking in bursts of rising pitch through the window cracked open to prevent condensation. The anchor line strains and shudders against its chock and the boat spins.

We came across the Gulf of Alaska yesterday from Seward in calm weather for our last whale research trip of the year, searched for orcas as we entered Prince William Sound via Montague Strait, photo id'd six humpbacks along Latouche Island, and met the front of the storm half-way up the strait as the clouds dropped to the water, as the wind sled-ded down the ridgeline of Montague Island to roil up the strait, as tiny drops of moisture fell, misting the boat windows. Before we anchored, we rocked in the chop off Point Helen getting the last cell phone recep-tion we'd have for days. This fall's storm was a triple-pronged monster. Three fronts were lined up in a row to the west, one a tatter off a tropical typhoon forecasted to drop a deluge of rain and blow forty-five.

One text message came through on my phone, from our friend Laura in Hawaii. We spend four months on the Big Island each winter, on a farm we share with Laura and her partner, Ralph—our homestead com-munity including also a flock of chickens led by an elderly, damaged-legged, goose-stepping rooster named Wally Ching; six African geese; a dozen Muscovy ducks; a herd of hair sheep; Ralph's pet golden pheas-ants; two aging cats; and a dog named Boo. The text said, "I think we're going to help Boo pass over today. He's failing rapidly now. Send prayers."

It seems it's a dangerous place for dogs, and a dangerous place to love dogs, that damaged piece of earth in Hawaii. Before Boo, there was a dog on the land who died of some kind of poisoning. By the time they got him to a vet, there was nothing anyone could do. His liver and kid-neys were shot. The same happened with Boo. The vet guessed his poison was an invasive weed, castor bean seeds stuck to his fur, pulled off with his teeth when grooming.

The water in Squire Cove is that fatigue green of dense-cloud days, as though the hemlock and spruce are leaching out their tints via the rain into the bay. To the north, where the wind slams down, the water's rattled with silver. The only contact we have with the outside world now is the VHF radio, and that is silent. Even the Coast Guard's occasional transmissions are garbled. Gone are the weekend boaters of summer, the commercial fishing fleet, the halibut charters. Our only news is the morning and evening forecast on the weather station, which we have to turn the squelch down to hear. So we don't know how it went with Boo yesterday. A couple days ago, he seemed better, but his kidneys never turned back on. The way with cancer a man like my friend Peter could be sound in so many ways—mind, arms, legs, heart—but when his liver went, none of that mattered. The things that make us look outwardly okay are just that—outward. Or maybe they reflect something true, a deeper okayness only the dying come to, if they're lucky. Like my friend Paula's radiance even in the thick of her stage 4 ovarian cancer. Mortally ill, yes, but she looked—how can I put it—*healed*. And I hope someday, like me, with my stage 4 breast cancer. Once in a while, I believe I'm getting there, an okayness with the process. I've struggled to react rightly to people's surprised "You look great!" when they haven't seen me in a while. Maybe it's safe and even honest to say, "You know, I actually AM okay." *But not in the way you think*. Maybe that's what Boo was saying that last day, when he wagged his tail at Ralph and Laura, when his ears perked up at the sight of a mongoose, and they allowed in a shred of hope that he was on the mend.

The day we first heard about Boo's sickness, we were still in town. It was a day we wanted to celebrate a rare bit of unexpected good news about my cancer, which we've lived with now for four years. My tumor markers were down, one number cut almost in half. Still high, but hell, you hold to what you can, though as a friend suggested the other day, you hold lightly. Craig and I got lunch at a café. I texted the news to my sister. But we kept relief on mute. It's been a year since my cancer came back, colonizing my lung lining and peritoneum, mutating genetically into two different forms. We know not to trust numbers. We know nothing lasts.

Which brings me back to Boo. The news of his poisoning came almost as counterweight to the cancer news. And though I approach the idea of prayer with the same caution as I do celebration or relief or despair at some shift in my cancer status, that was the day I started to pray for Boo. That was the day I pleaded. *I need that dog. Please don't take him away.* It's reflexive in me, having been raised Catholic by immigrant parents. Every night my mother recited our bedtime prayers with us, in Latvian, in the darkness. It's an old voice from childhood, the one that pleads—the same one that beseeched God to bring Serry back, for my cracked oboe reed to mend, for my cat Mince to recover from her spay surgery infection, for my sins to be forgiven while I knelt in the church pew after confession, mumbling my assigned Our Fathers and Hail Marys. That night we heard about Boo, I lit a Virgin of Guadalupe candle on our kitchen altar, and a beeswax angel candle I've saved for years for some special occasion. "Boo needs a miracle," Laura had said. I don't believe in miracles per se, but I kept the candles burning all night, as I do whenever prayer's all I can offer. Don't get me wrong. I'm a believer in my own way. What I mean is I don't believe anyone is more deserving of miracles or answered prayers than anyone else, and whatever is holy in this life doesn't work in that unholy, unjust way of granting some their wishes and not others. God's alleged mysterious ways—his/her inexplicable reasons for letting cancer take a child, for instance—hold no sway with me. I do believe each suffering being deserves a legion of candlelight, all over the earth, burning in his or her name, in times of trouble. I believe the gesture matters. So I do my part.

The next day, when Boo seemed better, but still hadn't peed, Ralph texted that he didn't hold truck with prayer, but that if Boo recovered, he'd become a believer. Ralph's a cynic. Every New Year's Eve, when Laura and I plan a ritual of burning and resolving and letting go, Ralph declares, "No more Mr. Nice Guy. That's my only resolution." So I didn't buy his bargain. The next time he texted, after Boo was dead, his first words were "Prayer is bullshit!" But I see through his cynicism. When our facades are stripped away, when our loves are taken without warning or reason, we are all kids crying for mercy, railing against injustice, stupefied and brought low by unanswerable *whys*.

Now that Boo's gone and prayer's no longer called for, I'm compelled to testify. Boo was part of what life on the farm was all about, a kind of joy, integral, like the trade winds and the rats stealing bananas off the racks hanging in the tractor shed, like the sound of Wally Ching's muffled hoot-like crows at dawn and surf pounding the cliffs in a storm. Like Serry, Boo was part husky, but mostly some kind of shepherd, with mixed-up eyes, one blue, one half blue/half brown. He had a mischievous way of sneaking ever farther onto the lanai evenings when we sat at the table jawboning after supper. He settled himself a few inches closer to us from his designated spot on the far east corner, hoping no one would notice. Ralph held no truck with Boo's shenanigans. *Get off the lanai*, he'd holler, and Boo would retreat to his corner and start over. Craig and I, we held a bit more truck. Too permissive, too susceptible to Boo's goofball face at our front door, which is half-window, staring in at us while we made supper. We were typical of aunts and uncles and grandparents everywhere, permissive toward what's not ours to raise to be well behaved and responsible.

I testify to Boo's shadow-shape loping across the grass in darkness from our house to Ralph and Laura's, to the warmth and solidity of Boo's back against the tent fabric when I camped on the bluff above the breaking ocean, to Boo's sighs in sleep letting me know he was there, that I was safe, to Boo bounding ahead of the car, white flag of tail-tip held high, welcoming us back to the land after we'd been gone, to his bad haircuts by Ralph giving him a too-big head for his near-shaved body, to his silly untrimmed tuft tail, to his always-peeling ugly nose. I testify to Boo beside himself when I sat on the bench to lace up running shoes, Boo recognizing my running outfit the minute I stepped out the door and getting wild, jumping up on me, Boo racing ahead, stopping to look back to see what the hell was taking me so long. Boo overeager to help herd chickens, making me scream *Bone-head!*, stubborn blockhead Boo scaring the birds, scattering them every which way, getting in the middle, and then magically driving the last one into the coop for the night. I testify to his being a mostly ineffectual sheepdog, not noticing they were loose till you whistled, pointed, which alerted the sheep so by the time Boo streaked across the grass to chase them, they'd already have ducked back under the electrified wire and stood watching him, with *damn fool dog* expressions on their faces. To Boo's houndish half-howl half-bay signaling a car's arrival or a wild pig in the night, to Boo chasing mongoose, the way he stotted like a transient orca leaping high above the waves after a fleeing porpoise, Boo airborne, his head swinging this way, that, to see which way his quarry fled, Craig and I urging him on saying "Jump-n-git-it, Boo, jump-n-git-it!" Singing "Boo-hitter, Boo-hitter" when upon opening the front door in the morning we startled him awake. Ralph's no-nonsense "Booya come!" and Boo hurtling up onto the lowered truck gate eager for whatever came next. All the calls from the neighbors a mile up the hill, "Hey you guys, Boo just showed up here," Boo and their dog Goldie growling and throwing each other to the ground in play just this side of violence, Boo dusty from sleeping under the house on hot days, Boo wading undaunted into tide pools, letting waves lift him and fling him against rocks, scrambling out and shaking salt from his coat, the way when I'd sit on the bluff staring at the ocean he'd sit there beside me staring out too, as though in commiseration or indulgence. I can't not testify in more detail to Boo's face at the front door window every night while we cooked because he'd grown accustomed to our singing "How much is that doggy in the window?" and then giving him a treat. Expectant that Craig would break a hunk of bread off a loaf, drizzle olive oil all over it, and give it to Boo, in direct defiance of Ralph's rules. A way we colluded with Boo against authority, like kids, giddy to be getting away with something. That's what Boo did to us and for us, most of all. Made us defy our own rigidity, take ourselves less seriously, give ourselves more permission.

For Boo, I testify to the same terrible grief I felt with the loss of our childhood pets, one after another, run over or diseased or shot or sickened, until Peaches, dumb and resilient enough to survive being hit by a car and being conked on the head by a frying pan, losing teeth so when he lapped milk he sprayed white all over the wall, Peaches our only pet who died of old age.

The day we heard Boo would die, we anchored the boat off Point Helen. Craig cut a thick slice off the loaf and drizzled on olive oil and carried it to shore in the kayaks, placed it in a mossy wet grotto in a rock face. It was a little like a shrine or an altar place, but darker. We stood back from it and Craig said that Boo was the epitome of joy, a reminder to take hold of that joy, because it could all be gone tomorrow. And then we took our basket and knives up into the woods and collected mushrooms, as a way of taking hold of something, taking hold hard in the moment. The wind blew the high parts of the trees, playing them like strings. It felt very much that we were alone in the sound. Summer over.

At first it's always a little frightening, that isolation, and then it's a relief and even a comfort. After that, with the storm worsening, we could easily have headed for the native village to shelter at their dock. We could have put our sadness more easily out of our minds. Maybe our friends Kate and Andy and their ten-year-old son Hawken, who live in the village, could commiserate, having had their share of pets, and then distract us with games of Uno. But both of us agreed we needed the quiet and solitude of Squire Island, and if that meant hurting harder over Boo, so be it. We knew Squire Cove would take us, sadness and all. So here we are as the storm howls.

Yesterday I finished the novel *We Are All Beside Ourselves Here* by Susan Joy Fowler. It's about a girl who grows up with a chimp as a sister, as a misbegotten science experiment. It was a true depiction of how close we are to animals—biologically and emotionally. They are our companions in the beauty and suffering and hunger and play of earth. In the birthing and dying. In cities, the lonely seek out duck ponds and park benches where pigeons scrabble at their feet for crumbs. Everywhere, people rescue injured birds. We are all beside ourselves when we exist beside animals. In this quiet cove, we claim to relish the solitude, but report every creature sighting to each other with the phrase, "Look, it's a little buddy." And feel less solitary. A harbor seal. A sea otter. Even an ordinary mew gull washing itself in the saltwater warrants a comment. Sometimes we prefer this to human company—wild animals, centered within their perfect boundaries, their sense of space.

Where Craig and I left the bread isn't too far from where, a few months earlier, on my fifty-first birthday, we'd watched a mother and two kit river otters preen and wrestle in the shallows. We hid ourselves behind a boulder to watch from above as they rolled and scrabbled and twisted their bodies among kelp fronds, as they moaned and harrumphed. Every once in a while, the mother glanced up, very much aware of us, keeping an eye. I called it my birthday present, that and the hour on the black sand patch where I did sun salutations, pressing my hands and bare feet among fresh otter, deer, and gull tracks.

River otters are predators, as was Boo, at the core. Once he took off after a wild pig. We screamed his name over and over, but he ignored us, consumed by instinct. We heard thrashing, Boo barking, a pig squealing. When he came back, blood spattered his chest. He was panting, and didn't make eye contact. The locals hanging out drinking beers on their tailgate looked impressed. A guy pointed his bottle at Boo, said, "You should train him to hunt pigs."

A window is a hole sawed out of a house. The holes in my house, in my body, started with Serry, and then there were more. The Irish setter stray who showed up at our house, and my sister and I right away begging, "Can we keep her?" and coming home from school to learn she'd been reclaimed and we had no chance to say good-bye, and the yawning raw-edged hole inside with no analgesic. Or the young golden retriever killed by a car on the busy road in front of our house. (No more dogs, my mother said, after that.) And my sister's kitten run over by our brother in the driveway. And my cat Mince who wandered off after botched spay surgery to die alone in the blackberry brambles. How it hurt, letting them go. Yet even alive, they would not be held, though we tried, my sister and I. At night, during bedtime prayers we clutched our kittens to our chests under the covers, and they squirmed to get away and then figured out if they relaxed and purred we'd release our grip and they'd make their escape. No one taught us to hold lightly.

Nothing could hasten the tight and hard way a skin seemed to heal over the hole, thin and fragile as a sheet of plastic tacked up over a broken window. Different kinds of holes opened when my brothers, seven and eight years older, left for college. I learned quickly that the joy of anticipation of their homecoming for school holidays was exactly equal to the sorrow of their absence when they'd leave. I'd learn, but could never damp down either feeling. Later, it made it hard to tolerate the thought of my mother embodying that child-shaped hole in her days when I left each time to return to Alaska. It's so much easier, everyone knows, to be the leaver.

The first hole I saw form in my mother was the one left by *her* mother. My sister and I sat in the back of the car, my mother in the front passenger seat, waiting for my father, who'd run into the smoke shop for the Sunday *Times* and his weekly carton of Marlboros. My mother didn't turn to face us when she spoke, so in my memory I see only the back of her head, brown hair neatly styled for church. She didn't turn, just stared out the window; otherwise I don't believe she'd have said it aloud. If she would have turned, she'd have remembered we were too little to understand. "You know, I just can't believe she's gone," she said. "Sometimes I feel like my mother. Like I *am* my mother." I was too young to put meaning to what her words described. Just a tatter off it, like a strip of fog snagged by trees broke free and lodged itself under my breastbone.

Much later, I felt it each time my stepkids came and went, two weeks on, two weeks off, between their mother's house and ours. The physicality of their absence, the material realness of it when I entered their vacated rooms ached, no matter that I knew they'd be back. More than absence, that vacancy was a negative pressure, a kind of sucking force, a vacuum. When I'd separate from my sister after a visit, the same thing happened. I realized some part of me was awakened, lured out of hiding, by that person, some dormant aspect, and I grieved not only the person's departure from my surroundings, but *my* departure. Can I make his loss hurt less if I try to be more like Boo, more goofball, more exuberant? No, the hole in me is only partly refilled by my own Boo-nature. I grieve the flesh-and-blood other. We *are* dependent. We can't be sufficient only with ourselves, no matter how fully realized all our aspects.

After several hours in the boat cabin as the storm intensifies, Craig and I grow antsy, our bodies cramped, our brains dumbed down from the low barometric pressure. I shut my computer and he puts down his novel. We layer on clothes and raingear and pull on rubber boots and Craig lowers the kayaks into the water. It's raining and blowing with fog lifting and lowering, erasing and revealing the spine of Squire Island above the cove. We beach the kayaks, drag them up past the tideline, tie them to alder branches, and set out, following a stream. A half hour into our hike, I am sweating, breathing loudly, steadily ascending, stopping to graze on blueberries, keeping an eye out for mushrooms.

As I crest a rise, a little ahead of Craig, I come upon a deer, a young doe. She stares, standing stock still, perhaps a hundred feet away. I freeze and stare back. I hold my hand up to signal Craig. I don't want to scare her. She has an unusual face for a deer, a little pushed in, her coat darker around her nose forming a mask. Her ears are enormous, perked straight up. Her eyes are enormous, dark brown. Her expression is alert, expectant, suspicious. When she licks her lips, I lick mine. I can see her instinct to flee come upon her, then give way to curiosity. She half turns and then whips her head back and faces me again. Craig creeps up beside me, and finally, she gives in to her innate caution, her wiser impulse, turns and takes a few high steps, then bounds up the tundra as if sprung, her legs tucked under her, white tail high like a flag not of surrender but of escape.

"Jump-n-git-it!" I cry. "Jump-n-git-it, Boo!" The words just come out, the ones I'd shout at Boo when he went after a mongoose.

The tundra is riven with deer trails, riddled with piles of deer scat. We follow them up into the fog, which no longer comes and goes but settles around the ridge and mists our eyeglasses. Craig ahead this time, he sees her first, grazing on tundra vegetation beside a good-sized lake, a granite boulder between her and Craig. He motions me over. Her head jerks up and again she stares. I step closer. She drops her head and nibbles reindeer moss. We drop to our knees, squat on our heels, and watch her. Because of the fog swirling around us, we can't see very far in any direction, so the world shrinks to one lake, one boulder, one patch of tundra, one deer, one pair of humans. As she moves off to the west we come after; then when she vanishes in a fog we follow her well-trod path. I am cold by then, and it's time to head back to the boat. We encounter her one more time. She bounds up a rise into the fog and that's the last we see of her.

I have orca-shaped holes in me, people-shaped holes, dogs, cats, an aunt, and a hole shaped like my cousin John. There's a big hole shaped like the Exxon Valdez oil spill, made up of thousands of holes the animals left when they died. There's a hole for my father, a hole for my mother. When I learned as a child that humans had shot Eskimo curlews and passenger pigeons to extinction, a vast hole opened up, and it's never healed.

I think we grow larger in this way. More filled with loss but equally with memory and even more than memory—more filled with our own realized selves, those parts that grew out like extra limbs, knowing intimately some other being or place. But not just knowing. Loving. Opening to.

The only way to be changed is to let another being (or place) completely in, to love with a wild, dangerous abandon, knowing the outline of the hole it will make is already being formed. It will hurt like hell later, but you let it come closer. Though you know the incipient hole is being carefully etched inside your body, in the place that houses your vital organs.

In a weird way, my body is riven with holes. My oncologist says, reading my PET scans, that my peritoneum is studded with cancer, lesions so small they can only be detected by their uptake of sugar and radioactive tracer. I think of the dense studding of the night sky with stars over our land in Hawaii. As a child I thought of stars as pinpricks in velvet behind which some unbearable brilliance was shining. In these four years with cancer, I've lost a breast, several lymph nodes, and the space between my right lung lining and my chest wall, which was sealed by talc. I have lost four friends, one aunt, and one cousin to cancer. I have lost the ability to run. I have lost lung capacity. I have lost denial of my mortality, and it's been replaced with knowledge that cancer will gradually take away various functioning parts of me until it takes my life. I am studded with all I have loved and lost and stand to lose. That's why it hurts, this life, and why I love it and want more. Why I can't help but hold on tight.

Today the loss of Boo settles deeper into my knowing. He will join other holes the land itself embodies. The sandalwood forest–shaped holes. The native bird–shaped holes. The Hawaiian king- and queen-shaped holes, and those of all the people. The Filipino and Chinese and Japanese sugar plantation worker–shaped holes. The dream-shaped holes. It's why the land feels not like paradise, but equivocal, fraught, beautiful, lonely, and vibrant, quiet and tired and depleted and dangerous. The earth is full of holes stippling the living weave. Like the pinprick holes that form in the rusting metal of something eaten away by acids. Or the wormtrack holes in mushrooms we find at Point Helen.

In a world like this, in bodies like these, equally presence and absence, equally living and dying, of course we pray. Prayer is selfish, but it's also selfless: it's enacted love, our way of showing we're in all this together. It's why I let my Baptist neighbors lay hands on me when I head to Seattle for some cancer procedure or other. I expect no miracles except the miracle of their actual in-the-flesh caring, their thin-skinned elderly hands holding mine. That is miracle enough for me.

In the sound, above my old research camp where I lived several summers as a grad student, there's an ancient hemlock my stepkids named King Tree. A cavity under its roots is filled with twenty-five years of offerings and mementos, like a reliquary. It's not far from our anchorage in Squire Cove, and I climbed to it the other day to wrap my arms around its shaggy, lichen-encrusted bark. The living King Tree exists side by side with the ash tree I loved as a child, which my father cut down when I was in Alaska. I take them both inside, the hole of one tree, and the wholeness of the other. In this way, my body and the earth's become exactly the same, equally flesh and absence, matter and antimatter.

All my absences surround me today as the equinox storm weeps out its rain and bluster, along with the living presence of Craig, a kingfisher, a deer somewhere up on the tundra, a hemlock, and a few wet gulls. And yet I'm nowhere near equanimity with it all. When cancer aches in my side, as it does at this moment from too much sitting, I do everything to push it away. When, during a symptomless lull yesterday, I turned to Craig during a mushroom hunt and exclaimed, "I feel so good!" I dug my rubber-booted heels into that moment. But this notion of being made equally of flesh and absence is a partial equanimity that might not be so difficult to enact. It's an equanimity I can live with, day to day. Because it's inside me, the truth of it—holes and flesh, all my loves, living and dead—and outside me, outside the window, around this stormy cove, everywhere in evidence.

Becoming Earth

Why do I need these landscapes? The image of the sea draws me out of my-self, forces all my attention to the surface so that I can cast my thought into the depths once again. As if an imaginative blow were needed for a longer, better-aimed thrust into the depths. . . . The roots of my astonishment at the world cling tight to my inner life, in a tangle of memories, experiences, atavisms from both my own childhood and that of our species.

—Anna Kamienska

IT'S APRIL AGAIN, AND I'M still here, and I still have cancer, and "the roots of my astonishment at the world" sink deeper than ever past last fall's leaf litter into the muck of breakup and resurrection. This year, spring is early in south coastal Alaska. Every morning I step outside, and the woods around my house are already awake, speaking through the throat clearings of varied thrushes, earliest of songbirds to arrive. On Facebook, people are reporting things like *one greater yellowlegs in Beluga Slough*. And *today I saw my first crane*. Just one is big news, gets a hundred Facebook likes.

Last night, Craig and I hiked around the Calvin and Coyle Nature Trail for the first time since fall, and a north wind blew across the wetland, pressed down on the dead, wheat-colored grasses, wrinkled the standing water. We were bundled up in scarves and hats. On the viewing platform, we could see ducks at the back of Beluga Lake through binocs. We heard Canada geese fly over. I'm not a serious birder. It's the sounds I'm after: it's mere presence or absence that matters to me now.

This town is filled with serious birders, people who can identify the peeps, the shorebirds of various species that for most of us are indistinguishable little mottled scurriers lifting from the mudflats into sheets-drying-in-wind flights. For me it's not about IDs, but the way the landscape, speaking in the winter tongue of branches creaking and resident birds—chirring natters of redpolls and pinched-lipped insistences of chickadees—gives way to these transient presences, these temporary inhabitants.

When I was younger, I kept a life list of birds. In college, I worked as a naturalist, and it was my job to name things, to know all the species of a place—the plants, the trees, the birds. In college, I studied botany, mammalogy, ornithology, ichthyology, dendrology, taxonomy. I learned to identify, classify. I learned stories: where the veery builds its nest, how the grape fern replicates its kind.

I was a twenty-year-old naturalist undergraduate student the spring I got pregnant—I can't even say by accident. I was an educated dumb fuck those days, lost my senses in an alcohol haze by night, regained my senses in classrooms and labs and woods and fields by day.

The other day, I started to burn old letters. A whole boxful. And certain journals, the ones from those college years. I sat in front of the woodstove and tore out journal pages and talked reassuringly to my younger self and said good-bye and stuffed the pages into the flames. I made a lot of ash this way. I was not without second thoughts and made a small pile of them to stash for later. The pages on which I'd written out my drinking and drugging stories, my love-lust stories, were interspersed with pages of field notes, sketches of great blue herons, poems to lakes, data gathered at beaver ponds for a project I worked on one summer. Something in me was trying to build a soul, and something in me was dismantling it, desperate for a man to keep me safe, for a high to make me feel alive. I'd like to claim the budding naturalist as my true self. I'd like to claim the woods as my true home, my actual safe place. I could tear out just the embarrassing pages and leave the nature bits, but who would I be fooling?

When you have metastatic cancer, you stop fooling yourself so much. You start to think about letting things go, including the old shames. You think about unfinished business and how to finish it. And if you can't finish it with people for whatever reason, you invent ways to finish it inside yourself. At the same time, you have present-tense business with the world, and it's the world outside me that pulls hardest. I have trails to walk and birds to hear and words to put to paper. The past, I realize, is embedded, within. The letters—the paper and ink—don't matter. Those people are inside—my past with them goes with me everywhere I go, along with the past selves I carry, the nature-girl and the druggie and the musician. I feel more and more like a tree, the way growth rings not only enumerate but depict, in a very crude form, the lay of the land, the good and bad, the years with and without sun or water, the years of stress and disease. The details, the stories of those years, are not discernible. They are secrets of the tree. It's what we call dignity.

The other day, on another trail I walk, a friend and I saw a black-winged shape about six feet up a cottonwood tree. From a distance, it looked like an angel. Up close, it turned into someone's glove. In another part of that cottonwood stand, we found a tree with a wound low down near the ground. A slab of bark was missing, revealing a near-white, pale scar, feathered with brown, shaped crudely like a pair of wings. Later, my friend sent me a translation of "Black Angel," by the Italian poet Eugenio Montale, which ends this way:

> great ebony angel
> angel dusky
> or white
> if, weary of my wandering,
> I clutched your wing and felt it
> crunch
> I could not know you as now I do,
> in sleep, on waking, in the morning
> since between true and false no needle
> can stop biped or camel,
> and the charred residue, the grime
> left on the fingertips
> is less than the dust
> of your last feather, great angel
> of ash and smoke, mini-angel
> chimney sweep.

I clutch life, feel it crunch. After burning letters, my fingers smell of ash and smoke. I realize, in truth, that an accurate journal of today would be similar to the burned journals of thirty years ago—nature as a steadying force in the path of a stumbling soul. You think you're making a soul, when it's not that simple. It's being made, and you're only partly the maker. As a child I was taught that the soul was given by God, unmarred. Each blot must be accounted for, confessed, and forgiven, the soul made clean again. As the soul, so the body, gifted, under my care. This is still my way. Only sometimes now the soul feels outside me, something I am trying to embody or become: this now blank white sky of thickened cloud growing grayer as the wind shifts to the east. If I stare at it long enough, it blots out my thoughts. Anna Kamienska put it another way: *The soul has two distinct layers. One is the "I"—capricious, fickle, uncertain, it hops from joy to despair. The other, the "soul," is steady, sure, unwavering, watchful, ready, aware.* Her definition of "soul" fits the sensation that comes over me when I'm alone in the woods. I become aware of a presence that is *steady, sure, unwavering, watchful, ready, aware*—pure life. Into that window, which I want to make a mirror, I stare and stare.

It's a paradox, two paths I walk. If to let go is to become one with earth, then the burning, the giving away, the throwing out. If to let go is to become one with earth, then the want, the walking, the seeds I plant and the plans I make, knowing they can be forsaken.

The year I turned twenty, in my college naturalist job, I walked with an older student the trails of a place called the Herbert C. Mackie Camp. The two of us sketched ferns, identified trees and plants, marked sites for interpretive signs, took notes for the field guides we would write, for nature hikes we would lead. The older student dressed the naturalist part, and she knew a lot more than I did about many things. She wore cargo pants and work boots and a fly fishing vest to hold her expensive binoculars and Rite in the Rain field notebook. A hand lens to examine fern spores dangled over her breasts. Her long blonde hair hung in a thick braid to her butt, and she slept with the guy who worked as a handyman at the camp. Not just slept with, they lived together. She was an adult, though only a few years older than I was. I was not an adult. Besides my sister and my boyfriend and the swamp, she became the only one to know of my pregnancy. She'd told me about her abortion. In the way of growing and dying things, she mentored me.

The names and facts I memorized on the nature trails that year didn't help me the day I peed on a stick and, with my sister, read the news it delivered. What helped me was the pull of place. After the shock, after the phone call to the older student, who gave me the number of the clinic I should call, I drove out to the nature center and I headed down the trail a couple miles through the woods, half-running for the swamp, and I sat on the ground at its edge and cried and listened to the swamp sounds that preceded and would continue on after me and wished myself into the heart of that inaccessible place, where creatures knew their purpose and carried it out unwatched. They did not question. They did not fail at their lives. I wasn't there at the swamp to make a choice; I knew I'd end the pregnancy. I wouldn't have been able to name my reason until much later. I went there to grieve, partly, yes. All my life I've grieved that child, though not the circumstance she would have entered. (*She*, then as now, is how I think of that life.) But perhaps I was doing something else there, compelled to that swamp, heart-pulled to a knowing I couldn't verbalize. I went there to gather my resolve. I went there to be witnessed and forgiven. The fact is, I acted out of a sense of survival, like any animal. Swamp child, I call her. I left the possibility of her in that place, buried her under moss, as I would one day, two and a half decades later, imaginatively bury my lost breast in a cove in Prince William Sound. What I didn't realize was that to let her go made her completely mine, internalized and eternalized, an inaccessible wetland I carried forward into the rest of my life, an ache reawakened even now by frog-croak, swan-bleat, crane-rattle. My body never carried any child but her.

The spring my cancer came back, two years ago, I walked almost daily the rickety boardwalks of the Calvin and Coyle Nature Trail to the viewing platform. Once, I heard the muted trumpet jazz riffs of swans ghosting through the spruce lowlands. I didn't know what was happening to my body at first. Over time, it had become harder and harder to breathe. I didn't know the lining of my lungs was gradually filling up with fluid from the cancer lesions growing and weeping there. I just knew I could no longer run or walk uphill: even the gentle incline of my driveway left me winded. Then as before, I went instinctively to standing water, to the flat, muddy reek of a trail winding through wetland, where almost no one else ever walked. The land trust that managed the trail had put up benches hewn from beetle-killed logs here and there, and I'd pause and sit to catch my breath. The day I learned my malaise was metastatic cancer, I walked the trail with my husband and a friend. It was June by then, and the swamp was flushed green. A doctor had drawn three liters of fluid from my lung lining in the emergency room, uncollapsed my lung, and I could breathe again.

I can't walk the trail without remembering. I ignore the interpretive signs placed at points of interest by the land trust, signs to explain the facts of this meadow, that stream. Memory of three springs has constructed its own signs in me, and those I read. One tells me to slow down at a particular bend of the boardwalk. I want to hear again the calls of swans I cannot see. I want to see swans at the back of the lake where yesterday we saw only mallards. My call not so different from the swans': *I want, I want.*

I've become less attached to names and facts, more attached to reasonless reasons, to the tug inside me telling me which way to go. The other day when I was driving to town, the wanting toward Prince William Sound, archipelago where I've gone to study orcas every summer since 1987 (except for the one summer when I was getting treated for early stage breast cancer), was so strong in me, I almost wept with its force.

In many respects, it's hard to know what to do with your life when you have a terminal illness with unknown terminus. You are no longer to be relied upon, as the disease's trajectory is cagey. You cancel out of things. You say yes with caveats. The median survival for metastatic breast cancer is two to three years. It's been over two years now since my metastatic diagnosis, five since doctors found cancer in my right breast. Each spring since then imprints a unique set of tracks on my map of where I've been. Who I am keeps revising. So I keep burning journal pages. I burn letters written by people who are now strangers to a stranger who was myself at twenty. This spring, I am burning and walking and planting seeds in plastic six-packs for another garden Craig and I will be planting. I'm spritzing the soil with water. This morning, the first green shoots broke the surface. I'm purging things out of my house, clothes mostly. I'm sewing old fabric into long strings of prayer flags and giving them away. I've consolidated my letters down to one box, from three. As time passes, I'm willing to give up a little more, and at the same time, I'm more wedded to things outside my body, outside my house, things from which my body—and perhaps my soul—is made: muck, swamp water, wind, birdcall. I used to try harder to explain these things to other people, but they are becoming less explicable. I'm hanging on, but not like I did to those men of my twenties, my holding tight with desperation, nascent and human.

There's desperation, but it's the desperation of cranes rising ahead of the first big fall storm to migrate. It's the pull, the want built into our bodies and the bodies of other animals. It's the desperation of spring, of nesting, of territory defense, of yearling moose driven away by their pregnant-again mothers. It's the want of these clueless juveniles so desperately baffled, the want toward who knows what. It's the want of diving creatures for air. Only my memory of the swamp—with its heron rookery tree, and the heron I watched that day stalking frogs, and its pileated woodpecker hammering through the quiet, and the day's heat rising in waves from the surface of stagnant water—feels still, held in suspension, its desperation so quiet, so hidden and inner it isn't sensed by the likes of me. It's the desperate resolve and the desperate grief I carried away.

Today the bare trees are a mess against the glaring backdrop of sun through thin high clouds, and the branches move in a cold north wind. They seem to scrape the sky and my face when I go outside to hang sheets to dry.

As I write, two swans fly past. Their long necks stretched out. *I want, I want.* I want to be the earth. They vanish into the broken light, urging me toward the place they are surely heading.

Epilogue:
Ever-Moving World

YESTERDAY, A BIG WIND CAME out of the north. Gusts sledded down the bluff behind our house and dove into the forest canopy. Every tentatively-holding-on yellow-gold birch leaf got swept up, tossed around, and flung down. Standing at the sink, I watched the air outside the window turn kaleidoscopic. The yellow-gold-spangled air whirled. The world williwawed in a yellow-gold storm. And then the air cleared, just a few individual leaves tipping this way and that as they drifted to earth. By day's end, the trees were mostly bare while the grass was covered in a bright weave of various yellows: amber, buff, straw, goldenrod, turmeric, ochre, agate, umber. The sky was bigger, more violet gray, taking up more space between branches. Wind blew wild through the night, and in the morning, though the temperature rose to fifty degrees and the wind was calm, the season had changed, is changing still, in the ever-moving world.

In Sogyal Rinpoche's *The Tibetan Book of Living and Dying* (my paperback edition with an autumnal goldenrod-yellow cover edged with an intricate saffron pattern), there's a chapter called "Bardos and Other Realities." On this morning after the day of leaf-fall, I open the book to that section because recently the word "bardo" appeared in my life. I'm a writer and teacher of writing. I'm a reader of spiritual, especially Buddhist, texts. And yet I didn't know this word "bardo" when our friend Ken said it at a pizza party the other night. Ken is sixtyish and has an impish yet sometimes intimidating face. His eyes are devilish, sparking with humor. His eyebrows are dark, prominent, mobile, and arched like the wicked queen's in the Snow White movie—the kind of eyebrows kids draw on faces of sinister characters. Yet Ken's all heart. The other night we were standing around in our friend's basement eating pizzas we'd baked in a wood-fired oven when Ken mentioned that the obscure term "bardo" had suddenly appeared in his life—twice in a matter of days. He said he first heard the term at the movies, a showing of *Dying to Know*, a documentary about the lifelong friendship of Ram Dass and Timothy Leary that had aired at our documentary film festival. And then, during a phone conversation with a long-distance friend, she dropped in the word "bardo," and Ken told her of the coincidence, and asked, "What are the chances of that?" As he prepped another round of pizza dough, Ken explained that the word meant "transitional state." In bed that night, I was reading a story in a magazine, and there it was again, the word "bardo."

It's an ever-moving world, and yet sometimes, we seem to be pinpointed at some kind of cosmic intersection, a crossroads, and a new concept enters, then changes, our lives. Another friend of mine says it's the universe, keeping its appointments with us.

I open *The Tibetan Book of Living and Dying* and read the first sentence of the chapter on bardos to ground myself more deeply in the traditional definition: "*Bardo* is a Tibetan word that simply means a gap between the completion of one situation and the onset of another. *Bar* means 'in between,' and *do* means 'suspended' or 'thrown.'" An ecological bardo is an ecotone, a transition zone between one biome and another, for instance the edge between forest and swamp. Such places in nature are dynamic, with greater species diversity than the zones on either side.

In the ever-moving world inside our minds, we navigate not by the present moment, but by the future. In that way, we're forever in transition. We venerate the idea of living in the moment, but we rarely slow down long enough to do it. I'm not a person who likes to make grand pronouncements, but the last week of my life, the first week of this October, it suddenly became very clear. It arrived, that knowing, like a poem, out of watching the leaves falling. *We live our lives almost entirely by the future. And we don't know it until the future is torn away.* It felt like a grand Truth.

But from this moment where I sit today, tapping at the computer keyboard at the kitchen table, I realize I'm looking at life from what feels at times like the inside of a bubble, my own biome. It's a very particular biome. I'm dying of breast cancer. Time no longer stretches forward from under my feet to the horizon—the future. Time—the unknown quantity I have left on earth, anyway—feels like a hoopskirt I wear, suspended from my hips, swaying, going with me wherever I go. So yesterday when I watched the leaves falling from the trees I love, my chest hurt. The dormant cycle of winter will give way to the unfurling of the most tender of greens come May, my favorite color. The forest will flush with green and birdcall, a happening that fills me with what I can only call ecstasy. It could very well happen without me. I know that nothing is lost in the scenario of spring except my anticipation of it, my own personal future tense, my taking that future for granted, that *spring will come, and you'll be here to see it.* I know, but grief gusts in anyway.

In June, a friend walked me home from another pizza party at our neighbor's house. The trees had fully leafed out, and we walked beneath a road-shaped opening in the green overstory of birches. I mused to him that I never saw birch saplings in this forest. When birches fell in winter, no young plants grew to fill in the gap they left behind, and I worried for the future of this band of woods uncommon in southcentral Alaska where I live, a region dominated by meadows, cottonwoods, spruce, and land cleared for houses with glorious views of Kachemak Bay and the glaciated mountains behind it. My friend explained that the birch forest was not stable. It was a transitional forest in our region. It would give way eventually to the climax forest of this place, which is spruce. In the 1990s, most of the spruce forest on the Kenai Peninsula, including my town, was destroyed by a massive outbreak of spruce bark beetles. Scientists attributed the outbreak's unprecedented scope (not the first in recorded history, but the worst) to a series of hot, dry summers, to a warming climate trend. In years after, fires swept through the landscapes of dead trees. Ecologists call this "disturbance."

Fire, flood, windstorm, land clearing, drought, insect outbreak, cancer. They disrupt the ecosystem, what we come to rely on as home, as touchstone, as body, as grounding. Communities on the Kenai Peninsula grieved the loss of our forest. They expressed grief through art, testimony, poems. Children who grew up in the twilight and shadows and sap-scent and wind-sough of spruce returned home from college to openings, grasslands studded with gray, bare, strangely sculpted snags, frozen in the position of their dying like victims of Pompeii. Windstorms broke them. Homesteaders logged them and heated their homes. My husband and I sided our house and laid down our floors with planks milled from their bodies. We knew the forest would someday grow back (and it is growing back), but we knew we would not live to see that climax forest again.

This week I've felt at times immobilized by bouts of grief. It took those falling leaves and it took a phone conversation with a friend thousands of miles away to mobilize it, but first, to identify the source of it. You might be thinking, well of course, grief. Of course it's there for someone dying of cancer. But immobilized grief feels different—heavier, more dense— than moving grief, wind-driven grief. Dying is letting go, increment by increment, of everything that has constituted your life. And when you think about it, that is a good description of living through time, too: shedding one thing, then another, from a placenta nub to baby teeth to adolescence to menstruation to hair. But when you die of cancer, death takes on definite form. Wind is invisible until a rush of falling leaves gives it form. We suddenly see the swirling, breathing, wild motion of wind. It's no longer an abstraction. You can't push it away.

With a terminal diagnosis, you get a certain measure of time to come to terms with the ongoing losses. You get a chance to say good-byes, to make amends, or to let go of what can't be amended. What matters most to you becomes acutely clear, and you shed extraneous things at an accelerated pace. Like that windstorm yesterday: the leaves were going to fall, but without the wind, they might have lingered up there for another week. The wind sped the process of shedding. Sometimes you grieve in anticipation of letting go of loved ones, places, jobs, abilities, possessions. Shopping with a girlfriend the other day, I sat on a bench in front of a display of shoes and boots while she tried on jeans. My abdomen was stretched by cancer fluid, and I felt imprisoned in my body. My eyes roved the wall, landing at last on an ankle-high boot with multiple straps in a pleasing shade of spruce green. I imagined wearing them with this or that pair of pants. I even checked out the price (expensive). But there was no impulse in me to try them on. Why buy a pair of boots I'd wear for perhaps a matter of months? What does a dying woman, who tries to give a lot of things away, need with new boots? Why spend $174 on a *thing*? Dying is letting go of things, turning toward intangibles, right? An oncology social worker I know would probably encourage me, as she does all her patients with cancer, to "live a little beyond your means." My sister would probably have egged me on to buy them, to treat myself. *You deserve it!* And it wouldn't have been wrong. But in that moment, I grieved for the way I used to live my life, blithely accumulating boots and baskets and books and publications and perennial plants without a second thought. I grieved the things of this world. I grieved my bootless, bodiless future, the loss of a future in which boots—and books, and objects, and collections of stones—mattered in my life.

Sometimes grief doesn't attach itself to anything in particular; it simply descends. It's weighted, not like leaves but like ashfall. Watching the trees get stripped, I grieved not for living beings, or things, or places, but for what holds all of it: the completely illusory idea of *the future*.

Physicists in the 1930s identified a "ghost particle" accompanying electrons, neutral in charge—the neutrino. A by-product of radioactive decay, neutrinos generated by nuclear reactions on the sun stream through the earth, our bodies, animal bodies, all matter, at a rate of billions per second, undetected, unseen. Without neutrinos, there would be no sunlight, no us. They are streaming through my hands, through the birch leaves, through the trunks and branches, through my cancer, and yet physicists little understand them, and the more they plumb, the more mysteries open outward. Writer Kent Meyers, in a 2015 article on neu-trino researchers in *Harper's*, writes, "I began to think of neutrinos and dark matter as whispers: the most intimate messages of the universe's voice, carrying its closest secrets to ears that are all but deaf—or perhaps more accurately, immune, because so other-natured."

Driving in the car yesterday, I listened to an interview on public radio with a neurologist who spoke of a ladder of intelligence. Humans, of course, stood at the top. The "dumbest" animal (his term) he could think of was an earthworm. Humans, he said, could be distinguished from all the other animals by their ability to tell stories about their lives. Some intellectual is always declaring what sets humans apart from other ani-mals. (Craig and I, having studied wild orcas for more than thirty years, have no patience for these distinction-makers.) Noam Chomsky claimed it was language. I'll bet someone claimed it was awareness of death, of a future. I bring this up because lately I've been watching a Steller's jay come once a day to my deck to feed on sunflower seeds I scatter on the railing. The jay stabs the seeds into one of my planters, which is made of a straw-like substance, storing them for leaner times—for a future.

Sogyal Rinpoche writes, "We can divide the whole of our existence into four realities: life, dying and death, after-death, and rebirth. These are the Four Bardos:

> *the "natural" bardo of this life
> *the "painful" bardo of dying
> *the "luminous" bardo of dharmata
> *the "karmic" bardo of becoming

I mean no disrespectful appropriation of Buddhist concepts (or tidbits of physics) for which I can claim only the most superficial of understand-ings. But for me, the experience of cancer has been a kind of bardo. Since cancer, I have lived my life in the presence of death, which is in a way like gardening as I usually do, but acutely aware that a brown bear is shuffling around in the brushy forest edge, fifty feet away. For two and a half years since my cancer came back in the lining of my right lung (and thus as stage 4), I've undergone various treatments to slow or temporarily halt the cancer's progression. When one treatment stops working, another is tried. In breast cancer chat rooms, women post comments and following their first name, you can see below it a list. It is the timeline, the abbreviated story, of their disease; the dates of its arrival and progress; and of the progression of treatment. The list begins with date of cancer diagnosis. The list does not begin with a birth date for the life of the woman, but a birth date for the life of her cancer. It is almost as though you've been reborn as a body with cancer, identity tied to its chronology. Here, for example, is how my cancer bio would look if I joined such a chat room:

Dx 04/10, Stage 2B, 2 cm, 5/15+ nodes, ER+/PR+, Her2-, 5/13 Stage 4,
dx mets to right lung pleura, ER-/PR-, Her2 equivocal
Surgery 5/12/2010 Mastectomy: Right
Chemotherapy 6/1/2010 AC + T
Radiation 10/15/2010 Breast
Hormonal Therapy 10/15/2010 Arimidex
Chemotherapy: 8/2013 Xeloda
Chemotherapy: 3/2014 Vinorelbine
Targeted Therapy: 3/2014 Herceptin
Chemotherapy 10/2014 Carboplatin + Taxol
Chemotherapy 8/2015 Kadcycla

There is movement here, but just looking at the list I feel claustrophobic, as though it seeks to trap me in its narrowly defined narrative—a story of me with cancer. The other day a friend asked if I'd checked to see if there were any innovative treatments for breast cancer available in Canada. I could devote my life to turning over every stone, and some people do. When I step back and imagine myself doing so, I see a woman circling a patch of dry ground, her eyes focused downward, stooping to tip over a stone, or kicking it over with her boot-tip, spiraling toward a center that never arrives. I want to live, and meanwhile the stream of neutrinos flows past and through me, on and on.

The Tibetan Book of Living and Dying describes a very foreign notion of dealing with one's physical suffering. Physical suffering, like the list of my cancer timeline, creates in me a bearing down, a narrowing of perspective, until I am a captive in my body. The other night, my belly hurting after a meal with friends, feeling as though I'd swallowed not the Moroccan lentils and salad but the forks and knives, I crawled into bed and opened the book. It described the practice of Tonglen. In our contemporary culture, we're encouraged to draw boundaries. We're scolded for martyring ourselves, for taking on the pain of others. *Listen*, we're told, *don't absorb*. As a child raised in a Catholic home, I knew nothing of contemporary psychology. When my sister had a migraine headache, I prayed God would give it to me. Jesus, after all, died for my sins. The Tibetan Buddhists express it differently. In Tonglen meditation, you imagine everyone on the earth who is suffering in a similar way as you, and you imagine breathing in all of their suffering, melding their tumors and their pain with yours, and breathing out healing to them. Breathing in pain, breathing out healing. You dedicate your personal suffering to the end of all suffering. Reading this in bed, it triggered my unease at falling into some old martyr complex. But I went ahead and tried it. I imagined others with metastases like mine, lesions oozing fluid into their abdominal cavities, caking up their intestines, wrapping around their stomachs. I felt them, women with ovarian cancer, people with breast cancer like mine, all of us in our beds, all of us on earth at the same time. I felt myself move out from my body, expand out of my personal story. Instead of feeling a growing burden, a burgeoning tumor load, I felt more space. When I stopped pushing it away, my pain opened, broke apart, like the autumn forest canopy after wind, fragments of sky bounded by the thinnest of branches.

The state the Tibetan Buddhists call "the natural bardo of this life" begins with birth and ends with dying. It's a transition from one transition to another transition, endlessly moving.

On cancer chat rooms, people often describe switching from one treat-ment regimen to the next as "failing." As in "I started taking _____ after failing _____." But a person cannot fail at chemotherapy, or at cancer. The disease in its late stages, like everything in nature, is a mov-ing target, ever evolving. But unlike many things in nature, unlike the human body, metastatic cancer grows stronger as it ages, as it mutates to evade treatment after treatment. It doesn't tire. It only dies because the body dies. My life has become intimately entwined with the life of my cancer. Does the date of my diagnosis mark my entry into the bardo of dying? Will I know when I get there? Will I know, intuitively, how to inhabit that state, how, like an animal, to move through it?

In art, I love the way form contains, compresses, holds, bounds. In an ever-moving world, we crave order: four seasons, four bardos, poems composed of couplets or quatrains, villanelles, sonnets, the seventeen syllables of a haiku. In high school, my piano and oboe teachers intro-duced me to the sonata, often a four-movement composition. It's inter-esting how audiences so want to clap at the end of a movement, even though the conductor keeps his one hand raised as he turns the page, even though the program lists the four parts as making up the whole. A movement ends with what sounds to us like resolution, yet it's not. The sonata is yet unresolved until the end of the last movement. It's uncom-fortable to sit in the gap of silence, the pause, the caesura, between them. Just as it's uncomfortable to sit in the silence of someone from another, less chatty culture or in the presence of the very old, or the dying. Study-ing poetry, I learned that half the poem was found in the silence. Robert Bly calls a poetry of intentional gaps "leaping poetry." The magic, the secret, is in those gaps, as much as it is in the words we land upon.

I loved the slow movements of sonatas best, and their terms: *ada-gio, andante, largo*. I loved (still love) music composed in a minor key. I didn't so much play my oboe as mourn into it, cry into it, sorrow into it, pour my incomprehension into it. Now I use words. My therapist, who's worked with me for the last five years, since the beginning of my cancer bardo, told me the other day that I must slow way down. "Make a moment into an hour," she said. "Make an hour last a week." Make a moment into a *movement*, I think. When around me people live in the future, this is not easy to do. Recently, friends began asking, "So when are you going to Hawaii?" Our proposed date two months away, what do I say? In the bardo of living, the future shapes our days, not the moment. We save, we plan, we bank on tomorrow, we mark dates in our calendars, we anticipate endpoints to projects and travel dates and submission deadlines. While we cut lemon cucumbers for refrigerator pickles, we anticipate picking up our daughter, taking her to tea after school lets out. We imagine the crunch of the pickle in the mouth of our son, the bitten pickle held in a paper towel as he stands before his math homework. The future creates form for us, and purpose. The moment is the boundless space.

This afternoon the wind picks up again and it swirls the leaves lying on the ground and on our deck. The leaves that remain high in the trees stubbornly cling. The alders that ring our yard remain green. Eventually, those leaves will wither and gray on the branch and clatter to the frozen ground like stiff fabric scraps. The wind has shifted to the southwest, and it drovers gray, light-backed clouds in a steady progression over the bluff and across the peninsula. The clouds seem to come from some endless source, out over the Gulf of Alaska. I know that stormy body of water is there, though the mountains across Kachemak Bay block it from view.

Winters, I've watched an oval of nearly tropical blue seem to form far out past the snow-covered peaks. It is the far edge of a cloudbank or weather front. I've longed for my body to be able to follow my eyes to find its source, out of whatever darkness fills me. I long for that clarity, though I will never get there. It is a place past the weather I'm experiencing, my now. The future is a place past the bounds of my own self.

"One of the central characteristics of the bardos is that they are periods of deep uncertainty," writes Sogyal Rinpoche. The bardo is "a continuous, unnerving oscillation between clarity and confusion, bewilderment and insight, certainty and uncertainty, sanity and insanity." He says that these oscillations create "gaps," spaces where "flowering" or transformation can occur. Instead, we move from event to event, passing right over the gaps. In the days when I felt immobilized by my grief at dying, when I felt outside of time, outside the future-driven human project, I lost my motivation, and it scared me. Everything slowed down, yes, but in a way that made me unable to get up off the couch except by force of will and inner scolding. *Push through it*, a voice in my head nagged. My time was running out, and I was filling it with nothing. I was in the gap, but unable to recognize it. I sat staring out the window for hours, watching the comings and goings of the birds who, in a matter of hours, ate all the seeds I sprinkled out. I rousted myself to give them more. If I couldn't participate in the project of furiously living on my own borrowed time, I could support it in other beings, make some small contribution to the whole endeavor: the frantic, gorgeous, agonizing bardo of living.

In all seasons, I've sat at this kitchen table writing, especially during the time between darkness and the sun cresting the mountains across the bay. In particular, day after day, I've watched one mountain, Grace Ridge, visible in an opening in the birch forest. It has a flat plateau that's called me like that blue imagined clearing in the cloudbank. One fall, I photographed the mountain every day, even when it was obscured by storm clouds. It was the longed-for place, a touchstone, like the mezuzah in my friend's entryway, which she reminds me to place my hand upon before I walk out the door. I climbed Grace Ridge three times in three summers, and then when I stopped being able to climb mountains, it became again an imagined place, a landing place for my eyes and mind. Its surface changed continuously. The weather passing over it came and went. But it felt unmoving, solid.

This time of year, snow falls on the mountain, then melts, again and again. Today it is stippled with white, the last snow dump partially erased. During that fall and winter years ago when I photographed the mountain every day and wrote about it in poems and an essay and dreamed about it and imagined it, I heard about a film called *My Mountain*, in which the filmmaker set up a camera on top of a mountain and filmed the weather and seasonal changes continuously, day after day. My imagination seized on that notion. My imagination became the camera that set itself on top of Grace Ridge. My imagination placed my own body on that flat tundra plateau and let the snow fall upon it, let it freeze up with the tiny tundra plants, let it thaw, let the wind blow over it, let it transform into bones, let voles chew it, let moss cover it. Even when I couldn't see the mountain, even when I was far away during the year I was treated for breast cancer in Boston, the mountain remained. Blueberries ripened and withered upon it. Strange bronze discs—boletes—sprouted upon it, then dried in the wind. Mountain goats trampled the slopes, grazed the vegetation. Marmots whistled from talus slopes. Storms came and went, the wind whipped up and died down.

I died. The words pop out on the page. I died and the mountain remained. I died and the baby leaves on the birch trees broke through their waxy casks in what was once my yard. I died and the nettles pushed up through layers of fallen birch leaves. I died and one day a wind came and the leaves blizzarded down. And the snow came, and the snow went. I died and you died and the ever-moving earth continued on and on. We died and the earth continued and changed. And so—living, dying, dead, reborn in other forms—did we. There is a future. It is beyond us, like that oval of blue behind layers of mountains, beyond weather. It is not ours to have or to hold. There is a future, and it is not us. It is the mountain. It is the earth.

ACKNOWLEDGMENTS

Thank you to the editors of magazines who gave some of the essays collected here a home out in the world: *Camas Literary Journal*, Winter 2015: "Ever-Moving World"; *Ecotone*, Spring 2013: "Nipple Unremarkable" and Spring 2016: "Becoming Earth"; *Orion*, March/April 2014, reprinted in *Utne Reader*, *We Alaskans* (*Anchorage Dispatch News*), and *The Week*: "Wild Darkness"; *The Sun*, August 2015: "Becoming Body," (published as "When No One's Watching,"); *Watershed Review*, Spring 2014: "49: The Last Five Days"; *We Alaskans* (*Anchorage Dispatch News*), September 2015: "When What I Feared Most Came to Pass."

For the tangible existence of this book, I thank my friend and editor Peggy Shumaker and Kate Gale and Mark Cull of Red Hen Press, for saying yes and yes and yes. I thank Mark Cull and his team for the artistry of the book's design. I am grateful for the generosity of Alexis Rizzuto for invaluable feedback on an early draft of the manuscript. I appreciate that my agent, Jeff Kleinman, reminded me that I was still a writer, even at the end of life. I thank Liz Bradfield and Christine Byl for encouragement around a Scrabble game one Hawaiian night when I was creatively stuck. I'm blessed that David Lynn Grimes sent, on what seemed like a whim but in hindsight felt like serendipity, the photograph that graces this cover.

I want to express special gratitude for all of the humans, animals, and places that populate these essays with me. I appreciate immensely the people whose faith in this writing allowed me to tell some of our shared stories. Through our experiences and conversations, my relationship to living and dying has deepened in ways it's impossible to enumerate. I'm especially grateful to my partner, Craig Matkin, for allowing me to reveal intimate aspects of our journey through cancer together in the service of truth; his willingness to let himself be vulnerable in these pages is astounding. I thank him also for the space he's held for my writing through thirty years of sharing our lives as friends, colleagues, and life partners.

Craig's support of me through the uncertainties and trials of breast cancer were buoyed up beyond measure by the love and loyalty of my sister, Mara Liebling. How to thank her for her presence, belief, and love over half a century's living? All I have is the simplest of words we learned as children, Paldies, mana mila Marite.

The essays in this collection were written over the course of five and a half years of living and dying with breast cancer, but they are the product of a lifetime of generosity. I will not attempt to trace their existence back to origins with the ultimate fortune of being born onto this incredible planet to live and learn. But my gratitude does extend all the way back, and to each of you who've touched my life by teaching me, protecting me, befriending me, believing in me, and supporting me, I send beacons of thanks. As these particular essays were written, I have been surrounded by a constellation of support: friends, fellow writers, colleagues, family members near and far, stepchildren, nieces and nephews, healers from many modalities, even strangers, also creatures. I have been held and healed by powerful places in the natural world, especially Prince William Sound; Cape Cod, Massachusetts; Bainbridge Island, Washington; Homer, Alaska; and Kapaau, Hawaii. Without this support, both of earth and of my human community, this book would not be. I would not be who I am. My most profound thanks.

Biographical Note

Essayist, poet, and marine biologist Eva Saulitis for nearly thirty years studied killer whales in Prince William Sound, along with her partner Craig Matkin. Her first book, *Leaving Resurrection: Chronicles of a Whale Scientist* (Boreal Books/Red Hen Press, 2008), considers questions science did not allow her to ask. Her second nonfiction book, *Into Great Silence* (Beacon Press, 2013), deals with the Exxon Valdez oil spill and the orcas she studied.

Her collections of lyric poems are *Many Ways to Say It* (Red Hen Press, 2012) and *Prayer in Wind* (Boreal Books/Red Hen, 2015). Her essays, poems, and reviews appear in many anthologies and journals including *Alaska Quarterly Review*, *Orion*, *The Sun*, *Northwest Review*, *Prairie Schooner*, *Quarterly West*, and *Crazyhorse*.

Her writing has earned awards from the Rasmuson Foundation, the Alaska Humanities Forum, and the Alaska State Council on the Arts. Eva Saulitis was associate professor in the University of Alaska Anchorage Low-Residency MFA program and a faculty member of the Kachemak Bay Writers' Conference.

Printed in the USA
CPSIA information can be obtained
at www.ICGtesting.com
JSHW082213140824
68134JS00014B/590